How Did You Find Me . . .
After All These Years?

How Did You Find Me . . .
After All These Years?
A Family Memoir

Dennis Vinar, Karen Vinar,
Jean Voxland, Andrew Voxland

MCP

Mill City Press, Inc.
2301 Lucien Way #415
Maitland, FL 32751
407.339.4217
www.millcitypress.net

Art direction and cover design assistance by Ronica Roberson, By All
Means Graphics, Northfield, Minnesota

Printed in the United States of America

ISBN-13: 978-1-54561-710-6

Dedication

We dedicate this piece of family history with love to:

- Our children: Jean, Stacia, Chandler, Kyle, and Tristan
- Our grandchildren: Terra, Laura, Hanna, Ryland, Raya, Aspen, Kaden, Victoria, and Phoenix
- Our great-grandchildren: Audrey, Stella, Gretta, Jack, and Margaret

Contents

PROLOGUE
Dennis

If it were not for what transpired on October 25, 2014, this book would not have been written. On that particular evening, I was at a dinner party with some friends of mine. A woman, a friend of the host of the party, stood up and asked if we wanted to play a game. We all said yes. She said: "If your primary physician gave you sixty days to live, who would be one person you would want to take to Starbucks or take out to dinner, or with whom you would just like to talk? As the question went around the room, people were pondering choices ranging from politicians to movie stars. It came to me and, without hesitation, I said, "Karen Lehmann." Then came the questions from my friends.

"Where does she live?"

"Don't know," I responded.

"Who is she?"

"My junior high and high school sweetheart."

"Is she married?"

"Don't know."

"Does she have a family?"

"Don't know." And then I finally said, "You asked questions. I gave you the answers. This is all I know."

So the next day, Sunday afternoon, as I was sitting in my favorite chair watching the Minnesota Vikings, a friend of mine asked me to join him on the networking site LinkedIn, so I did. I saw the search bar, and I thought about the previous night and said, "Why not?" I felt mischievous, so I typed in "Karen Lehmann." Her name and picture appeared in the third position down on the results screen. I clapped my hands together and said, "That's my lady!" to no one in particular.

On LinkedIn, I found that she worked in Everett, Washington. So I waited until one o'clock in the afternoon, or eleven o'clock in the morning in the state of Washington, on Monday, and called her. The receptionist would not put me through to her.

The receptionist asked, "Can I take a message?"

I said, "Yes. Tell her an old friend of fifty years ago called. My name is Denny," and I gave her my phone number. The receptionist sent a text message to Karen (as I learned later), and within minutes Karen called me.

Her first words were, "How did you find me?"

"Oh, whatever happened to 'hi,' 'hello,' 'how are you?'" I joked.

We quickly covered the basics. We were both single. I had been divorced for years, and Karen's husband had passed away four years earlier. I eagerly asked her, "What airport do I fly into if I were to come to see you?"

She said, "Seattle."

"I'm flying out tomorrow!" I responded.

"No, no, no. Not so fast," Karen said, then very hurriedly added, "We need to get reacquainted first." I could hear the humor in her voice.

Since Karen was at work, she couldn't talk long. She asked if she could call me back after she got home from work that night. I told her she could call me after 8:15 central standard time because I had to go to an AA meeting.

That was the beginning of a three-month-long electronic court-ship. We would text, e-mail, or talk on the phone daily, but we did not see each other until January 20, 2015. Two days later, we were married, after which I asked: "Now that we're married, can we go out on a date?"

The love story you are about to read began in 1959 in a rural Midwestern town about fifty miles west of Minneapolis when a young man of fifteen became attracted to a young girl of thirteen.

I was outgoing, and Karen was reserved and one of the smartest kids in school. I worked on a mink farm to have money so we could be together. We knew that what we had was not infatuation. So many people thought we were crazy to say we were in love at such a young age. How did we know it was love? We felt it in our hearts. We both took, as we called it, "the eighteen-inch journey from our head to our heart."

It's amazing how our life experiences and the choices we make, along with past family traits and our heritage, make us into the people we become.

Chapter 1: 1959 – Our First Christmas
Dennis

I look out of the window of my bedroom after waking up, and there is snow everywhere. It seems really cold outside. I can tell that the snow that started yesterday morning has left its mark. It's Christmas vacation, though, and I don't have school today.

My dad breaks into my thoughts as I am lying in bed. "Dennis, how would you like to make some money today?" he asks from my bedroom doorway.

"I am only fifteen, so I am always up for earning cash, Dad. What are you thinking?" I respond quickly, already becoming more alert.

"All that snow that got dumped on us last night needs to be removed from all the cars in the sales lot. How about you come to work with me today and help clean up? Dress warm!" he says, turning away and heading off to grab some breakfast. Dad sells cars for a Buick dealership in St. Paul, and I can imagine the extra help would be appreciated on a day like today.

"Sure, Dad. Sounds cool," I call in response. As I hurry up and get dressed to ride to work with him, my thoughts first revolve around the cash I will make and then turn to Karen, my girlfriend—who, I think, is absolutely fabulous. Maybe the money will become a Christmas present for her.

It's really cold working in the car lot. After a while, I barely have any feeling left in my toes. I've even gone into the office to warm up, but my toes seem to be permanently unyielding. My hands are stiff from the cold and shoveling the snow I was asked to remove. It seems like the snow in the car lot is never-ending at times, but my mind is focused on that brown-haired girl with a sweet smile back home.

Work isn't so bad when I think of Karen and what I might be able to afford for a Christmas present.

It's the end of the day, and my pay has been given to me—cash which is now burning a hole in my pocket. All I can think about is getting a Christmas present for my girl.

"Dad, I know you are in a hurry to get home, but can you make a stop first?" I ask.

He looks at me. "You already want to spend that money you just made, son?"

"Sure do, Dad. Can we stop at the Sears and Roebuck store on Chicago Avenue and Lake Street in South Minneapolis?"

"Sure."

All I can do is smile. I'm motivated to see what I can find for Karen. Dad pulls up to the store and stays in the warm car, allowing me to go in by myself. I'm not exactly sure where to look, first, but I decide to look at clothes. Clothes, jewelry, scarves, and gloves all seem like items that would make good Christmas gifts. As I contemplate all the choices in the store, I know my favorite is clothes, because I enjoy looking nice myself. I flip through the clothing racks and consider skirts, blouses, and jackets, but it is the sweaters that catch my eye. *Wow, I really like this yellow one. I can see Karen in it. She would look fantastic in this sweater,* I think to myself. *This is the one. This is the gift.*

I do not even consider the fact that most of the money that I earned is going toward one gift. Purchasing the yellow sweater for my sweetheart has made me feel euphoric. I run out into the parking lot where Dad is waiting with the car running and the heater turned on.

Dad looks at me and says, "Did you get what you want?"

I answer, "You bet, Dad. Thanks for stopping."

"You got any money left over, Son?"

"Not much. It was a special gift."

"What the heck did you buy?"

"A yellow sweater for Karen," I say, and I smile.

Dad looks at me sternly and declares, "You took your hard-earned cash and spent it on a girl."

"Yes, I did, Dad."

The ride back to Brownton is quiet. We don't talk much to each other. I know he is upset that I spent most of the money I had earned on Karen, but my excitement to give her the sweater outweighs any other feeling. I know it is a special sweater.

Brownton Public School   Brownton, Minnesota

Chapter 2: 1959 – The Yellow Sweater
Karen

In a small town of 695 people, most everyone knows everyone else. We go to the same churches, shop at the same grocery stores, and all the kids go to the same school. It is easy to know who everyone is.

I have a favorite guy. I am in awe of him. He's named Dennis Vinar, and he's fifteen. He was held back due to a childhood illness, so he is one year ahead of me in school. He is *so* so attractive—and popular with the girls. When we started hanging out together last year, the girls were kind of jealous. Dennis is a real dapper dresser, always wearing the latest fashionable attire. He has an outgoing personality and an everlasting smile. I love the twinkle in his eyes when he smiles at me. He makes me feel so warm inside. He always carries a comb in his pocket to comb his hair frequently so as to not have a single hair out of place. I giggle now as I think of it, but when he combs his hair it reminds me of the song lyrics "Kookie, Kookie, lend me your comb." It was easy to fall for his charm, and we began spending much time together in the last year.

Dennis is so nice, and he walks me home from school carrying my clarinet for me. Once we reach my house, we usually stand by the back door and kiss and talk until he has to hurriedly leave me to go to football practice. This fall he was late for practice quite often—I wonder why the coach even kept him on the team. Perhaps it was because he could run fast. I smile whenever I think about him running. *He is so cool!*

There aren't many activities in our small town to keep my friends, well, all of us school kids, occupied. We frequently join our friends after football and basketball games to drink cherry Cokes and eat French fries at the local hotel restaurant and play the latest tunes on the jukebox. Tonight, I went over to the jukebox to put in my dime and chose the song "Dream Lover" by Bobby Darin. It is one of my favorite songs to dance to with Dennis. I also love to dance to "Put Your Head on My Shoulder" by Paul Anka.

"Dennis, I just put in a dime for a great song. Do you want to dance?" I ask him.

"Oh sure," he says. He takes a swig of his cherry Coke and grabs my arm.

As we dance, he looks down at me and asks, "Did you have a good day?"

"Yes, I did. I got an A on my algebra homework, and I am real happy about that." I smile. "I also feel really good about the song we are playing in the band right now. We should be really good just in time for the Christmas concert. How about you? Did *you* have a good day?"

"I am coming to your concert, Karen. I wouldn't miss it for anything," he says. "Yeah, basketball practice went well; I got in some good lay-ups. Maybe I should have you help me with my algebra, Karen." He grins at me and winks, and then just holds me a little tighter.

As we dance to the slower songs, I relax in Dennis's arms and think about how happy I am right at that very minute. My friends are here; I am with Dennis; and, I chose some of my favorite songs on the jukebox. The French fries and cherry Cokes always taste better when I am with everyone here.

I like to wait for Dennis in the school hallway while he showers and dresses in the locker room after basketball games. Then we walk to town holding hands. At evening's end he walks me home, and we stand on the back steps of my house holding each other, not wanting to leave each other—until one of my parents turns on the outside light. This is a signal that it is time for me to come into the house. Dennis then walks the mile and a half to his house at the other end of town.

This year is our first Christmas together. I am lying on the sofa looking at the lights of the Christmas tree that my parents, my sister, and I put up during the last weekend. The house is quiet tonight. It is easy to hear my parents softly laughing about something in the kitchen. My grandmother has gone into her room to knit, and I am not sure what my sister, Roxanne, is doing. I am trying to read a book for my literature class, but my reading gets interrupted by the ring of the phone. I can hear my sister answer and then say, "Sure, I will get her. Karen," she calls, "your boyfriend is on the phone." I immediately lay the book down on the sofa and run to the phone.

"Dennis? Hi . . . ," I say breathlessly.

"Hey, hon, I have a surprise for you," he says.

"What is it?" I ask excitedly.

He laughs and says, "I am not going to tell you. You will just have to wait and find out, won't you? What are you doing tonight? Some of the kids are going to the Brownton Hotel for cherry Cokes and Christmas dancing. Do you want to join us?"

"I would love to, but let me check with my parents, first, to make sure they don't need me for anything," I say.

"Call me back, and let me know. I will bring your Christmas surprise over to the house with me," he says in a teasing tone.

"Oh, sweetie, can't you tell me? I am so excited; I can't wait," I declare.

"Ask your parents, and then call me back," he says as he laughs.

I chat with my parents, and they don't have anything special planned for me, so they are fine with whatever I want to do. When I call Dennis back, he won't tell me anything about the surprise, and I am so excited. He says he will be right over.

When I hear the knock at the door, I know it is him, and I dash to open the door. I open the door and let in all the December cold along with my super-handsome guy.

"Hey, nice Christmas tree!" he says as he walks into the living room. "It's the perfect place to put a special present for a special girl!" He grins his exceptional smile, and I melt inside when I look at him.

I look at the box he places under the tree. It is all wrapped, and I want to open it really bad, but I don't. "You don't want me to wait until Christmas, do you, honey?" I ask with a little tiny whine.

He doesn't say anything at first. He just stands there and looks at me. My parents are still in the kitchen, and we are still in front of the Christmas tree. He bends his head down and kisses me in front of the tree. I feel like I am floating. "No," he says softly, "you don't have to wait until Christmas." He bends down and picks up the box and places it gently in my hands. "Open it," he says.

"I am not going to argue," I say with a smile. I tear off the wrapping paper, and the gift is in a box. I slowly open the box, and in it is something wrapped in tissue paper. I unfold the paper, and in the paper is a beautiful yellow sweater.

It is the most wonderful sweater I have ever had. I know I will keep it forever. I want to always remember our first Christmas. I put on the sweater right away.

"I will wear it tonight," I say to him. Then I look at him and say with a warm smile, "Honey, I love it. I will keep it forever!" I love the look he is giving me.

"You look beautiful in that sweater, babe," he says with emotion.

Wearing it makes me feel like his arms are wrapping around me, bringing me warmth and comfort. Gosh, it is so special.

Chapter 3: 1960 – Worn-out Shoes
Dennis

Basketball season is underway, and we have just arrived back in Brownton from winning an out-of-town game. The bus is noisy with everyone talking excitedly about the game. The air is festive in the bus, and all the kids are talking about going to the restaurant in the hotel. Hunger is the topic of conversation among most of us guys, and I realize that I am hungry and decide to join them. We get off the bus to walk down the street to the hotel, and I find that my feet are cold.

When we arrive at the restaurant, I look down at my shoes and feel embarrassed when I realize that I am wearing my black-and-white saddle shoes. After all, everyone knows you don't wear black and white shoes in the middle of winter. To make matters worse, my right shoe's sole has a hole in it, so before I left the house for the game, I took some cardboard to cover up the hole.

Once inside, I see Karen and her friends at a table across the room, but I can't make myself walk over there. Instead, I talk to a few of my friends and then move to the pinball machine. I want to talk to Karen, but I can't get rid of my self-conscious feeling. I don't want her to see my worn-out shoes.

I stand all evening at the pinball machine so no one will take notice of the worn-out shoes on my feet, but as it gets later, I know that I want to walk Karen home. I see her and her friends get up from the table to leave, and I move to walk out the door with her.

"Hi, Karen," I say, trying to curb my self-consciousness.

She grins back at me. "Hi, Dennis. I am glad you came over to say 'hi.' I was wondering if you would come over and talk to me."

I respond with, "Mind if I walk you home?

"Of course not," she says when she smiles up at me.

Karen waves goodbye to her friends, and, once they have their backs turned, I grab her hand and hold it as we walk all the way to her house. I don't feel cold when I am with her because our love is so strong and comfortable. As we walk side by side, my mind is totally on her. I don't pay any attention and don't even notice the snow in my worn-out shoe.

We arrive at Karen's house, and we stand on the back doorstep like we always do. "Honey, do you want to come in?" She encourages me with a smile. Hoping she doesn't notice my shoes, I slip them off at the back door. She invites me into the living room, and we settle on the sofa for a couple of kisses. Then her mother walks in, and I know it's time to go home.

As I walk the mile and a half home, I reflect on the night. I remember the game and how excited everyone was. Unfortunately, remembering how cold I was when we walked from the bus to the hotel—now that Karen is home and warm—I am cold once again. Ashamed of the hole in my shoe, I make a vow to myself as I walk along: I will never again have worn-out shoes.

The next day, Karen and I drive to Hutchinson to buy me a pair of shoes. As we drive there, I ask, "What color shoes would look good?"

She responds, "Brown loafers."

Little did I know that some day I would have some thirty pairs of shoes for all seasons—with all the soles intact.

One morning, as I am slipping on my winter coat to walk to school, my mother corners me by the front door.

"Dennis," she says, looking at me, "Can you please stop by the Red Owl and pick up some milk on your way home from practice today?" My mother shops for groceries at Lehmann's Red Owl grocery store, where Mr. Lehmann writes her purchase amounts in a little book.

I think of Mr. Lehmann and his daughter, Karen, and the possibility that she just might be there. At this thought I grin back at my mother and respond, "Sure." This is one errand I will be really glad to do!

School goes slowly as I sit in my classes. I look at the clock, and the hands are moving at a snail's pace. I can't concentrate this afternoon. My thoughts are revolving around walking Karen to her next class when the period ends, and then picking up milk at the Red Owl. It isn't the actual act of getting milk that I am thinking of, though, because I am daydreaming about the grocer's daughter. I see Karen at school in the hallway and walk her to class. My heart just picks up its pace a little bit every minute I get to spend with her. She makes me smile.

After basketball practice, I run down to the Red Owl and dart through the glass door. I scope out the shop looking for Karen, but I don't see her. Disappointment shoots through me. I walk slowly over to the refrigerated section and pick up a gallon of milk for Mother. Since I don't have any money for the milk, when I go to check out, I ask Mr. Lehmann to add the milk to our tally, and he adds the milk to our family charges in his little book.

I am disappointed that I didn't get to see Karen, but Mother will be happy that I brought home some milk for dinner.

A few weeks later, on a Friday night, I am picking up Karen to go to a dance at the high school after the basketball game. I am really looking forward to going out with her after the game. She always makes me feel terrific.

I stand at the door of her house and knock. Mr. Lehmann answers, looking very serious.

"Dennis, I would like to talk to you," he says.

I have to admit I am worried a little bit because of his serious expression. For a moment, I wonder if he is going to tell me not to take Karen out on our date.

"I know you work at the mink farm," he says. "And your parents' bill at the grocery store is at about one hundred dollars."

I think about this sentence and the pointed way in which he is looking at me. Gosh, one hundred dollars is a lot of money. I am standing in front of him, and I am not sure how to respond, but I remember that I have money in my bank account. "Mr. Lehmann," I say, looking him in the eye, "I will pay the bill tomorrow."

Karen walks into the room just then, and even though the hundred dollars crosses my mind a few times during the rest of that night, I concentrate on her and enjoy the dancing.

The next morning, I am supposed to go to work at the mink farm. Instead, I go to the bank and draw out one hundred dollars from my savings account. I don't necessarily feel good or bad about what I am doing, but I know I am doing the right thing for my parents and the family when I walk across the street and pay Mr. Lehmann one hundred dollars toward my parents' grocery bill.

Months later, the morning sun wakes me up, and I still feel tired. I stare out the window at the fall colors on the leaves in the yard. I have to get going to get to work at the mink farm. As I lie in my bed, my mind rewinds the memories of the past spring and summer. The past months have been so great. Karen and I have spent a lot of time together, even though we know people think it is just dating and that we don't have deep feelings for one another. They think we are too young, but we really do love each other. I think about her all the time. The dances after the football and basketball games in the school lunchroom have been a lot of fun. We've danced to slow music like "Slow dancin', swayin' to the music, slow dancin', just me and my girl" by Johnny Rivers. I love holding her in my arms while dancing to those slow songs.

1960 has been such a great year. I asked Karen to my junior prom in the spring, and she said yes. Prom was great. She looked so beautiful that night. During the year we have attended prom, homecoming, and all those dances in the gym. I enjoy thinking back on all the time we have spent together.

I remember a warm, sunny summer day. I was walking to Karen's house to see her, to hold her gently, and kiss her. After I arrived at her house, we went for a walk around Brownton and happened to walk by the red brick City Meat Market. We found a spot where we could carve our initials in the brick—just like thousands of other people had done in the past. We carved "DV+KL". From the meat market wall, we held hands and walked to the Brownton city bandstand. From there, we walked to the Barney Tadsen baseball field and watched the Brownton Bruins play a rival team from Stewart. As we held hands walking, we talked about our future together. After each of our walks and talks we would stop and give each other a gentle kiss, and I knew then that I was with the person with whom I wanted to spend the rest of my life.

Some Sunday afternoons, before I got my driver's license, we would walk to Weert's Drive-In to sit outside on their worn, painted picnic table to have a Coke. We would then walk across the street to my house. When we were alone in the house, we would go into the living room to watch TV and laugh. If we wanted to neck, I would pull closed the sliding door between the dining room and the living room, and that time would be ours. After leaving my house later Sunday afternoon, we would walk to Karen's house. Once in a while she would pull my arm, look into my eyes, and say, "Kiss me."

I got a 1952 two-tone green four-door Ford this summer. We like to go to drive-in movies in Buffalo Lake, Hutchinson, or Glencoe. When we get there, we sit in the back seat and make out, not really watching the movie on the screen in front of us. It is our time to be together. We have been together for several months now, and our making out in the back seat is leading to more. Our making out has led us to explore one another's bodies—and it is getting difficult for me to keep my hands off of her.

I need to get out of bed and stop my summer reminiscence.

I get dressed and go downstairs to hear my older brother teasing my ten-year-old younger brother. Walking past two of my three sisters, I ignore their chatter. As I sit in the kitchen grabbing a little bit of breakfast before going to work, and listening to all the family banter, I remember how special our time together was the night before.

It's October of 1960, and last night—the homecoming dance—was fabulous. The gym was decorated real neat for the dance. It was cool to be crowned homecoming king in my junior year, but that wasn't the best part of the night.

Karen and I walked out to our car after the dance, and as she slid over to sit next to me in the front seat, I put my hand on her leg and started to move it up her thigh, but she stopped me, saying, "Let's go to Lindy's Café in Glencoe to get something to eat." Later, when we got back from Glencoe, we stopped to park in a secluded place, and she put her hand on *my* leg and said, "This is a non-wrinkle dress." My heart skipped a beat. That's when I knew I was home free.

It seems that now that we have committed to the act of making love—and, yes, it is "making love" and not a "wham-bam-thank-you-ma'am"—there is no way of keeping us apart. We meet each other in the hallway between classes at school so that I can walk her to her next class. The only time we're apart, other than in class, is at lunch, because Karen walks the two blocks to her home where her grandma is waiting with lunch ready, watching *As the World Turns*, her favorite afternoon soap opera.

We "park" at a local man's airport, or else on a country road next to a farm that everyone calls "Lover's Lane." We make love a lot in my '52 Ford, and on Sunday afternoons in my parents' house, and on the sofa of Karen's parents' living room.

Chapter 4: 1961 – A Tough Decision
Karen

Reflections of last spring, 1960, are running through my mind today with visions of Dennis running at his track meets and baseball games, our walks from school, and the school dances and parties. We went to his junior prom together. I love my dress; it is a soft grey-blue with yards and yards of fabric in the full skirt. It was so fun to twirl the skirt around when we danced.

Dennis got his class ring and asked me to wear it as a sign of our devotion to each other. Of course it is much too big for me to wear it on my finger, even with a lot of tape wrapped around it, so I wear it on a chain around my neck. I love to show off the shiny gold ring with its ruby red stone center. Everyone in school knows that we are a couple.

Our plans for summer included spending as much time together as possible, taking long walks or rides in the country, going to movies, sharing milkshakes at the local drive-in restaurant, and just hanging out. Dennis even got a car, so we could go to drive-in movies or secluded roads to park and listen to the radio.

As I look back on the summer, we attended many baseball games at the local ballpark, but we couldn't concentrate on the game. We would go underneath the grandstand bleachers to kiss and hold each other. In the fall, our intimacy grew quite strong. I remember thinking: "I know I am young, but I am in love."

This past Christmas was really wonderful. We enjoyed the holiday lights and festivities with our families and each other. Dennis was so wonderful; he gave me a red manicure set this year. I love it so much. I will always treasure it.

We are now into the new year, 1961, and I haven't been feeling well the last couple of weeks. I have missed a few periods, so my mother has accompanied me to the doctor's office for a checkup.

The doctor walks into the room and looks at his clipboard, but he doesn't meet my eyes when he first walks in. It is very quiet in the room, and I am suddenly nervous.

He looks up, meets my eyes, and says, "Karen, you, my dear girl, are pregnant."

Oh, my gosh! . . . I can't believe it. I am pregnant? No, this can't be happening to me.

I stare at the doctor and say, "No. The test can't be right. It must be mistaken."

The doctor looks at me and pointedly says, "Young lady, I am not mistaken," and he turns and walks out of the room.

What am I going to do? I am only fifteen. This is definitely not in my life's plan. I want to go to college and become an interior designer. I read a book from the library about an interior designer and thought that, with my artistic talent, it would be a good career for me. What am I going to do now? I have a little problem.

I guess my problem isn't so little, is it? It's pretty big, and this makes me feel totally devastated.

Later, at home again, as I sit in my bedroom thinking about the whole doctor visit, I contemplate taking my own life to avoid the embarrassment for my parents and Dennis. How can I even tell Dennis about this?

"Karen?" I hear my mother at the door of my bedroom.

"I am not sure I want to talk, Mom," I say with a strained voice.

"Your father and I want to talk to you," she says. "Come down to the kitchen."

I dread this conversation, but know I might as well get through with it. I sit down slowly at the kitchen table where my father is reading the paper.

He says, looking at me, "Your mother told me about your doctor appointment today. We have discussed your little predicament, and we just want you to know we are going to help you. We need to discuss your options though."

I slowly nod my head.

"We will work something out, Karen," both of my parents console me. Mother comes over and lays her hand on my shoulder for a little bit. I am comforted, a little, by her hand. "But we do need to talk about the options here," my father says. "First, you could have an abortion, but your mother and I are not leaning that way since it is illegal and would be hard to get."

I kind of cringe when I hear him say this. I don't even really understand what an abortion is. Oh—I know what it is. I am simply not sure what they do, and this thought makes me scared.

My father continues, "We can all raise the child together, but we don't feel that is a very good option either. The last option is for you to have the baby and give it up for adoption. We have heard that there are places in Minneapolis where you can go, continue with school, stay there, have the baby, and then give it up. A nice family will come and adopt your child. Then, once you have the baby, you can come home and finish high school." My father gives a small smile as he says that last part.

"Dad," I rush to say, "what if Dennis asks me to marry him?"

My mother cuts me off right away as I say the word "marry" and exclaims, "Karen, definitely not! You are not going to get married at the age of fifteen. You are going to graduate from high school—and then college, if you want to do so. No, you are not going to get married." She wipes her hands absentmindedly across a dishtowel.

"But, Mom, I am in love with him!" I cry out. "I want to be with him. I know he loves me too!"

My father cuts in and quickly says, "All you feel is puppy love, Karen. Yes, he is a nice boy. He is a hard worker, but you are not in love—and you are not going to get married. I think your best option right now is to go away and have the baby. Give the child to a couple who can't have children of their own. It's the most logical thing to do."

As I sit there listening to him, my mind says, right away, Yes! I can have the baby, and then give it to someone else. I know I don't want to necessarily keep a baby. I do want to finish high school and then go to college. It's important to me. I really do want a career. But I don't want to go away. I don't want to leave Dennis and my parents. I don't want to leave my friends. I don't want to go someplace to be with a bunch of pregnant girls.

A sliver of a thought enters my mind, and I realize that my parents could be a lot worse. Here they are, probably embarrassed, yet trying to be supportive and help me make a tough decision. I am so lucky to have supportive parents. The only thing wrong is that even though they are giving me options, I feel like there is only one choice I can make. I feel cornered. My fifteen-year-old mind understands, but I also have feelings that I can't necessarily describe. My subconscious feelings might have something to do with not wanting to give up a baby, but whatever they are, the emotional feelings are overwhelming, and I can feel tears sting my eyes.

As I sit there with my parents looking at me, the tears fall down my cheeks. This is it for me. This is not what I wanted, and now I am petrified. My mind is spinning, and I see Dennis in my mind: I see his smile; and I all I want to do is see him.

"I need to talk to Dennis. It's his baby, too," I say and get up from the table to go back to my bedroom.

A little while later, as I wait for Dennis to pick me up for a dance at the high school, I rehearse in my mind what I want to say to him.

I hear his knock at the door and run to answer it, calling over my shoulder as I run out, "See you all later." I get into Dennis's car, and we don't talk too much at first. When we arrive at the high school, I put on a fake smile and try to concentrate on him.

I realized, when I was getting into my dress, that I am starting to show a little. I hear someone say in a light-hearted, teasing tone, "Now, all you thin girls, get out there—get out on the dance floor!"

Dennis turns to me and says, "Karen, get out there; go out to the dance floor."

I squeeze his hand and respond, "I have gained weight; I can't." Instead, we leave the dance and go to the car.

It's cold outside, but it's nice just being with Dennis. But I also know I need to tell him. As we drive north out of town, he pulls into one of our favorite spots to park. He turns the car off and pivots in his seat to look at me.

"Honey," Dennis says as he looks at me, "is anything wrong? You look kinda funny."

"I am fine, but I have something to tell you," I say, looking away from him. I want to tell him, and then I don't. I don't want him to get scared and leave me. I have heard stories about other girls who have told their boyfriends things like this—though maybe not as serious as having a baby. The guys get scared and run.

"What is it?" he asks. He touches my shoulder. I turn to look at him.

"I have missed a few periods. I wasn't feeling very well and went to the doctor. The doctor told me I . . . ," I pause because I just don't know how to say it, ". . . I am pregnant." Again those dreadful tears fall down my cheeks.

I must have stunned Dennis. He is speechless. He reaches out to me and pulls me across the seat so I am sitting in the crook of his arm. We sit there, staring out the window, for a long while. I calm down for a bit, and we are both lost in our own thoughts. I feel the rush of tears again.

When I start to cry, he says, "Honey, we are going to get through this. We can get married. We can keep our child. Things might be rough at first, but I know we can do it."

"Sweetie, I love you, and I want to get married, but there is no way my parents will allow me to get married. They say I am too young."

"What is going to happen, then? Where will our child go?" he asks with tears in his own eyes.

"Mom and Dad say there is a place in Minneapolis where I can go to have the baby. And, when I come home, I guess I'll just go back to life the way it was. They are going to find out more details from our pastor," I say, gloomily.

He turns my shoulders so I am facing him. "No, you are not going away! No way! Absolutely not! You are having my baby, and no one is going to send you away." He hits the steering wheel with his palm. I look at his eyes, and they are not teary anymore. Instead they are glittering. I can feel his frustration.

"Oh," I say, then swallow hard.

My head is buzzing; it hurts. I lean back against the seat and close my eyes. I can feel the tension of our conversation radiating throughout the car. I want to go home and crawl in bed and sleep. I think of sleep.

Dennis turns forward in his seat again and puts his arm on the back of the seat and around my shoulders. We sit in silence for a minute, and he says, "Sorry, sweets, I am just frustrated. Our timing isn't good here, is it? We were playing with fire, and now we've been burned." He leans over to me and very tentatively covers my mouth with his. His kiss is sweet and tender.

He moans softly, "Karen, I don't want you to go away," and we continue to slowly and softly kiss. "Marry me, Karen. Marry me," I hear him say.

"I am sorry, love," I say softly. "You know Mom and Dad won't let me get married to you."

With that said, the rest of the night is quiet, and we don't stay out long. Dennis drives me home, and I go to bed early.

Last week Mom, Dad, and I met with the pastor of our church. He gave us the number for Lutheran Social Services in Minneapolis and said they could help us in making our decision.

My parents took me there for a visit, where I was interviewed and accepted, assuming I choose to have the baby and make an adoption plan. They said I could move into one of their homes for unwed mothers in March or April, but I insisted that I want to complete the school year, which isn't over until the end of May. Lutheran Social Services said that, in that case, I can move into the home in June and spend the summer there until the baby is born, and then go back home to school in the fall.

I have it planned, and today I have to break the news to Dennis.

"Honey," he says right away, "marry me. We can run away somewhere to live and raise the baby together."

I respond sadly, "Love, we don't have any money. How could we possibly do that? My parents said marriage is out of the question. We are both too young and have our whole lives ahead of us. My parents think raising a child at this age would be too difficult for us and they will not give us permission."

The conversation ends unhappily, and Dennis leaves me on my own.

I am going ahead with my plans to finish the school year. Then my parents will take me to the home for unwed mothers.

Chapter 5: 1961 – Apart and Very Lonely
Dennis

I t's spring 1961, and tonight we have just left a high school dance. Earlier tonight, one of the guys from the senior class was asking for the thinnest girls to come out on the dance floor so that he could throw them around a little and show off his swing dancing talents. I was standing next to Karen and her friends, and I said, "Karen, you should go out there onto the dance floor; it would be fun." I looked at her and smiled, but she squeezed my hand and said rather quietly, "I have gained weight; I can't."

We leave the dance after that and walk to the car together. We are sitting here in my car, spending the evening together. It's cold, but we keep each other warm in our arms. Karen has just told me why she didn't want to go out onto the dance floor tonight. Her weight gain is due to an unplanned pregnancy—she is carrying my baby. "Stunned" might be too easy of a word to describe how I feel right now. It's definitely a shock, but when I ask her to marry me, she says "No." She looks at me with tears on her cheeks and says, "There is no way my parents will allow me to get married. They say I am too young."

My heart feels like it is being torn in two. Seeing the tears on her cheeks breaks my heart. I am having a hard time grasping the fact that my girlfriend is carrying my child. Mine. *My* baby. There must be something I can do. There must be something *we* can do.

About a month after the dance, I am with my family enjoying Mom's roast beef for Sunday dinner because my older brother Duane and sister Valoris are both home for a visit. I love our dining room table, especially when it is full of roast beef, carrots, mashed potatoes, gravy, and homemade kolaches made from Grandma Vinar's recipe. The table is surrounded by my family. It is a tasty meal, and my three sisters, three brothers, mom, dad and I are all enjoying it. My dad clears his throat, and we all look at him rather expectantly.

"I got some news this week at work. I am going to be working at the St. Paul Ford dealership, and your mother and I have decided to move out of Brownton. We bought a house in Minneapolis, and we will be moving in a few weeks. The drive will be better for me, and the move will be good for your mother." He looks at all of us sitting at the table. My older brother is the only one who doesn't seem really surprised at the news. I don't know what to think.

"Dad," I say, "I am going to be a senior this fall. I only have a year left."

"You don't have a choice in the matter, Son," he says with a tone that means "don't even bother talking to me about it because my mind is made up."

"Dennis, you will be fine," my mother says. "Everyone likes you, and you will make new friends quickly."

My sister Sharon responds with, "Mom, what about me? I don't want to leave my friends. I can't leave now." There is resentment in her tone as she continues, "We have all kinds of fun things planned for senior year." I know how my sister feels about going to a new school. She is a year younger than I am, but due to a childhood illness I had, my mother kept me back a year. We are both going into our senior year.

My father says in a stern voice, "There will be no more discussion about this. We are moving. We have already purchased a house. There is nothing to talk about. You two seniors will be completing your senior year of high school in Minneapolis."

There is not a lot of conversation around the table after that. While everyone is cleaning up the Sunday dinner dish clutter, my older brother touches my shoulder and asks, "Hey, you okay?"

"Yeah, I'm fine. Why are you asking that kind of crazy question?" I ask.

"Well, you know . . . ," he hesitates and then says, "You know why Dad and Mom are leaving Brownton, right?"

I think about this for a minute and then say, "Wait, . . . do you mean to tell me they are leaving Brownton because of me? Because I got Karen pregnant? Man, nobody really knows. She isn't telling anyone."

"Well, yeah. What did you think they would do, Dennis?" he asks. "That's a big burden to place on Mother. People talk. People gossip."

"Man, you are not making me feel good right now, brother."

"I wasn't intending to make you feel bad, Dennis. Just stating facts—and I want to make sure you were okay.

"I don't have a choice, do I? What is done is done. I can't go back—but I wouldn't want to go back either," I say.

I walk back into the kitchen, look at my mother, and ask, "Is there anything else you need, Mom?" She looks me straight in the eye, and there is an exchange of communication between us that doesn't need words. She gives me a hug, and I go outside to throw a baseball with my younger brother.

In a small town, you grow up hearing all the town gossip, but you never think at the age of seventeen, you will become part of that gossip.

One Saturday morning, I walk into a local hangout to have a burger and fries. I walk to the end of the bar and place my order. While waiting for my order to come up, the owner leans over the bar and whispers in a low voice "Did you get the Lehmann girl pregnant?" I tell him to keep the hamburger, get up from the stool, and walk out.

One of my classmates says to me one day, "How's your pregnant girlfriend?" In a split second I get angry, throw him down the school stairs, and keep hitting him in the face until a couple of buddies pull me off of him.

At the mink farm where I work, most of the full-time employees have no more than an eighth-grade education, and they say to me things like, "I hear you got a girl in Brownton pregnant," and other things that shouldn't be said in polite conversation.

With every negative comment that is made about Karen, I get more and more angry, but I also feel sad for her. I always wear my emotions on my sleeve, even when we go to a drive-in movie, where I weep at the sad parts.

It's summer, 1961, and I miss my girl. She has gone to an unwed mothers' home in northeast Minneapolis, and my family also moved into Minneapolis this summer. I am living with my parents, and maybe this is a good thing since I'm not alone like Karen, but I am not happy. At least I am closer to Karen.

I left Karen to ponder her three choices, and to make her own decision. One choice was to get an abortion. The other two choices were either keeping the baby or putting the baby up for adoption. Karen chose the last one and, after the school year ended, moved to the unwed mothers' home.

So now we are both in Minneapolis, but I am not allowed to see her very often. I miss her a lot. I go for long walks around Powderhorn Park and think of Karen. How I wish things could be different. I just want to be with Karen.

They have pretty strict rules at the home where Karen is living now. Our meetings must always be supervised and scheduled. I can't just call on her. Everything has to be pre-arranged because we are under age. I am six months short of being eighteen years old.

If I were eighteen, I would be keeping our baby. I know that Karen wants to go to college, and I know she could finish college, even while being with me. I have three sisters, so they would be able to help me take care of both Karen and the baby. If I were only a little older.

Chapter 6: 1961 – Summer Away from Home
Karen

School is out for the summer. It's June, and my parents are driving me to the home for unwed mothers in Minneapolis. Dennis was not invited to come along. My dad pulls up in front of a very non-descript, two-story house in a residential neighborhood. There are no signs or evidence indicating that this is a home for unwed mothers.

A woman answers the doorbell and ushers us into a rather stuffy sitting room where she introduces me to the five other women who live in the house along with the housemother. It is explained to my parents and me that there is a schedule and a routine we have to follow that includes chores, doctor's appointments, and visiting hours.

I hate saying goodbye to my parents when they leave. I feel alone. I know I am not, but I still feel it inside.

The daily routine of cooking and eating meals together, completing the assigned housekeeping duties, and going to doctor's appointments is broken up with various activities to pass the time. Several times I try to learn how to knit from one of the women living in the home, but embroidery is more to my liking (little do I know that I will never embroider again after the summer ends). There are books and magazines available for us to read and craft supplies to help keep us busy, but time seems to drag on very slowly. I wish I could be with Dennis to go to a baseball game or a movie or a summer picnic, but he is not allowed to visit me without arranging it in advance.

My roommate at the home is several years older than me, but we have many long talks during our time together. Her nickname is "Sarge" because she was in the army before getting pregnant. Her boyfriend left her when he found out she was pregnant. I am happy Dennis didn't "walk" on me, and that I am still able to talk to him—but I worry what will happen to our relationship in the future when I go back to Brownton. I desperately want our lives to go on as they were before I got pregnant.

"Do you want to go for a walk?" my roommate asks.

"We have walked to the park and back twice today already," I respond.

"I know, but what else is there to do around here?" she whines.

"We could listen to some music on the radio."

She turns on the radio and "Take Good Care of My Baby" by Bobby Vee is playing. "How appropriate!" I say and then start to sing along. After the song ends, I ask, "What kind of family do you want to take care of your baby?"

Sarge ponders this question thoughtfully and responds, "I hope they have other children in the family. I don't want my child to grow up as an only child. I think it's important to have siblings."

I have a sister seven years younger than me. I don't know if she knows that I left for the summer because I'm pregnant. Because of our age difference, we are not real close—even though we share a bedroom. She has her friends with whom she hangs out, and I have my own friends—and Dennis, of course. (Many years later, I will learn that my sister was nineteen years old before she found out that I had a baby at fifteen.)

One of the doctor's appointments that I remember most from my time living at the home is with a psychologist (or a psychiatrist) who determines through some stupid test he makes me take that I got pregnant on purpose because I hated my parents and wanted to get even with them. Nothing could be further from the truth—I love my parents. I try to convince him that I love my boyfriend, that the pregnancy was an accident, and that we are just too young to start a family at this age. Even so, he will hear nothing of it.

Day by day, the summer drags on with us women waiting patiently, or not so patiently, for our babies to be delivered. We take walks to a nearby park and talk among ourselves to ease the loneliness we all feel. We are given the chance to go to the Billy Graham Crusade and also go to an occasional movie to break up the monotony.

Although we don't worship together as a group, we are encouraged to attend church services on Sunday with family members if possible. We sit at a table together at meal time and give thanks for the food and the day. Devotional material is always available for those who choose to participate in group or individual prayers. I'm not sure we all believe the same way or if we are all of the Lutheran faith, but we profess to be Christians together. God is on our side in our decisions and our lives. We know with His help, our children will be sent to loving and caring families. This belief gets me through the days I spend in the home.

My parents come to visit me a few times on the weekends. On one of those visits I ask Dennis to come over to join us to go for a ride and get an ice cream cone. It is a day that I will always treasure. I am finally able to spend time with Dennis, even if it is only for a little while.

Chapter 7: 1961 – The Phone Call
Dennis

I t's Sunday afternoon, and I'm just hanging out with my parents and thinking about Karen, the baby that is yet to be born, and starting school in a new city. All of this for the hundredth—or maybe even thousandth—time, when I hear the phone ring. One of my sisters answers the phone and says, "Dennis, you have a call." I walk over to the phone, pick up the receiver, and find that it's Karen on the other end of the line. My heart quickens a little bit.

"Hi, Karen," I say, exhaling slowly. She hasn't called me since she has gone to the unwed mother's home. I am so excited to hear her voice and am trying to keep my emotions under control.

"Dennis, my parents are coming over this afternoon. I could really use your support today. Is there any chance you could join my parents and me?" she asks.

"Of course," I respond quickly. I'm thrilled at the thought of seeing her. It's been a long time since our last visit. "Karen, I'm so glad you called. I miss you so much. How are you feeling?" I have been thinking about her so much that the concern in my voice is audible.

"I'm fine, but I miss you, too. I would really like some ice cream," she says. I can tell by her voice she is smiling, and I know we are going to get ice cream. At this point, I just want to make her happy.

"I will be right over, sweets," I say and hurry out of my parent's house to drive over to the home.

It doesn't take me long to drive the five miles from my house to hers. The song "Dedicated to the One I Love" by The Shirelles starts playing on the radio, and I reach over to crank up the volume. I feel like there is a song in my heart just because I got to hear my girl's voice.

I arrive at the home after her parents, and find the three of them visiting in the living room. I am ushered in and sit down with Karen and her parents. We make some small talk, and then her father suggests we go get ice cream. Karen and I sit in the back seat of her dad's beige Plymouth, and I want so badly to hold her and to kiss her. It's painful to sit next to her in her father's car and not be able to touch her or hold her. It would be nice to just comfort her and say the things I want to say. As much as I love being with her and her parents, I keep wishing for some time alone—just so we could hold each other and talk.

We arrive at the Dairy Queen, and I look over at Karen, give her a wink, and she winks back. We both love ice cream, and I am remembering a time during the last summer at the Starlite Drive-in just outside of Hutchinson. Before the movie started, Karen and I walked over to the concession stand and bought a root beer float with two straws. I don't remember what movie we watched, but it was the best root beer float I ever had.

Karen's father asks me what I would like to order, and I have a hard time choosing. I am not hungry; I just want to be with Karen. But I choose the chocolate Dilly Bar, and Karen orders a banana split. She says to me with a grin, "Whatever I don't eat, you can eat, Dennis."

The four of us take our ice cream treats and sit on the picnic table in front of the Dairy Queen. My Dilly Bar is dripping down my fingers because of the summer heat. When I lick the ice cream off my fingers, I look at Karen and she giggles. I struggle with my words because I want desperately to be alone, but I don't want her parents to know just how much. I am wishing I could walk her home from the Dairy Queen.

Our time together is too short—definitely not long enough for me. I head home after the ice cream with the same thoughts whirling though my mind, and again I think, If only I were eighteen. If I were eighteen, I would keep my baby, and I know we would make it through the rough patches. We would make our life work somehow.

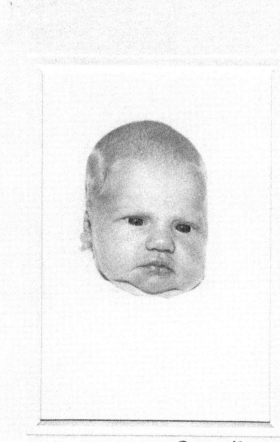

Chester Freden

Chapter 8: 1961 – Baby Girl
Karen

Early on Sunday morning, August 13, 1961, I am awakened by light contractions. The housemother takes me to the hospital where she stays with me through the next few hours, comforting me until my baby girl is born.

Later, in the hospital, I don't remember the actual birth. Maybe I was sedated too much to remember it, or maybe I am just too traumatized with the ordeal to want to remember it because I have to give up the little bundle that Dennis and I created together.

I need to call Dennis. I want to give him the news myself. I also want to ask him if he wants to sign the birth certificate. There is a phone in my room so I dial Dennis's number.

"Hello," answers someone from the family; I can't tell exactly who it is.

"I'd like to speak with Dennis, please," I say rather breathlessly.

"Sure" is the response. I can hear a muffled voice on the other end telling Dennis he has a phone call.

"This is Dennis," I hear him say, but my words seem to get stuck in my mouth.

I slowly respond, while tears glisten on my eyelashes, "Hi, love, it's me. I just had our baby."

He doesn't respond right away, and then I can hear the awe and exuberance in his voice. "I will be right there! Are you okay, honey?"

"Yes, I am fine. Dennis, we had a girl. I named her Denise DeeAnn, after you. Do you want to sign the birth certificate?" I ask. I can't help but give a little smile.

I can hear a catch in his breath, and then he says, "Wow. I am coming in to see you, honey. I want to see you and the baby." And then the line is disconnected.

I also call my parents, and they, too, say they will be there in the afternoon. The nurse asks me if I want a photo of the baby, and I say yes. I know that I will treasure that photo in the years to come, because it will be all I have to remind me that this chapter of my life ever actually happened.

It is wonderful to see Dennis again. I haven't seen him since we had ice cream with my parents that Sunday. The nurse comes in and hands the baby to him. I am so happy that Dennis is able to hold Denise before we have to hand her to the nurse and never see her again.

I realize then, even though I had almost shoved the thought out of my mind, that once you have carried a baby inside of you for nine months—even if you give her over to the care of another family—she will always be a part of you.

I am not sure how to handle the range of emotions that is going through me right now. I am happy to see Dennis but kind of sad to see his face as he holds our baby. Then I realize this is the only time I will ever see or hold the child that is a part of me—and a part of Dennis. I wonder if I am going to have regrets, but I do feel I am making the right decision. The path Dennis and I have chosen at this crossroads is the best for all of us: me, Dennis—and the baby.

September arrives, and I go back to school as if nothing has happened, greeting my friends with a smile and happy to have "the incident" behind me. Do I think about Dennis and Denise? Yes, of course I do, but I made the decision to give up the baby, and there is no rethinking it now.

My junior and senior years of high school are devoted to studying and participating in as many extracurricular activities as possible—band, chorus, the school yearbook, and the school newspaper—just to keep my mind off of Dennis and our daughter.

I hear rumors about Dennis occasionally, but I do not try to contact him—and I never hear from him, either. (Though, I learned later, he did try to reach me, but my family never told me.)

As my senior year of high school ends, I am named valedictorian. I am focused on college, where I plan to finish my degree in four years and then establish myself as an interior designer.

Chapter 9: 1962–1963 – The US Army Wants You

Dennis

Spring 1962.

It's graduation day, and of course I am happy to be free of the classrooms, but now I need to figure out what I want to do with my life. I have been thinking of joining the Army but I'm not real sure that is the direction I want to go. As I sit with my classmates during commencement, I see the faces of family and new friends, but not the face I would love to see in the crowd. Karen is the one person who could really make this day one of the best of my life, but I think that by now she is probably with someone else; maybe it is for the better. Sometimes I even think and feel it was just a fling.

As I think of Karen, I think of the baby. Our baby was born at 10:35 AM on August 13, 1961, and put up for adoption. Karen named her Denise DeeAnn after me. That was proof, to me, that Denise was conceived out of love. For a fifteen-year-old girl to name the baby after a seventeen-year-old boy, it had to be love. It couldn't be anything else.

As my mind wanders during the commencement ceremony, I realize that our baby is ten months old now. I wonder what has happened to her. I hope she is being taken care of well.

1962.

After completing high school earlier this year, I have been lying around not doing anything. I still can't see Karen because her parents won't allow it. My dad came home one afternoon saying I should get up and get a job.

I was walking down Lake Street in Minneapolis one day and saw the sign for the Army saying, "I want you," so I enlisted. It's nice to finally be eighteen and able to do something on my own.

My first sixteen weeks of training are in Fort Leonard Wood, Missouri. In my second eight weeks of training, on a Saturday morning, the captain of our unit calls me to stop by his office after our Saturday inspection. What in the world could he want? I ask myself. I can't think of anything I might have done wrong.

I open the door to his office and move to stand in front of his desk.

"Vinar," he says, "the US Army received a letter. The letter states that you got a girl pregnant when you were living in a small town in Minnesota. Do you know what I am talking about?"

I look at him solemnly and answer, "Yes, I do."

"Well then, Vinar, as long as you are in the service, the US government will be deducting a fifty-dollar savings bond from your pay check to cover the cost of the baby." He tells me, "This deduction will go on for thirty-four months. There is nothing you can do about it. I just wanted to relay that information to you. Dismissed." I can't believe it. The seventy-eight dollars per month that I earn will be drastically cut with fifty dollars taken out.

Before long I receive new orders stating that I am going to Germany. The captain tells me I should take a trip home to touch base with my family before I ship out. Before I leave, though, the guys ask me if I want to go to Waynesville, Missouri, to get drunk—and I say yes.

We walk into a bar and my friends proceed to find a couple of ladies of the night—prostitutes who charged eight dollars, plus two dollars more for the room. The guys also want to get tattoos and have their girlfriends' names tattooed on the top of their left shoulders.

They almost convince me to put "Karen" on my shoulder, too, but I choose not to do so—just like I choose not to be with another woman.

After that night, I go home to Minneapolis for two weeks to visit my family.

During those two weeks I try to look for Karen. The last time I saw her was in the hospital. I think about her all the time and really want to talk to her and let her know what I am doing. I had heard that after she graduated from high school, she had started attending the University of Minnesota in Morris, Minnesota. I am not sure whether that is what she is doing, but I hope so. I have no way of finding her. I can't even call her to tell her I am going to be out of the country for three years.

So, here I am, leaving the States and heading off into the military. I continue to think about her as our ship leaves the dock. I stare out the porthole of the ship and look down at the water passing below me.

I wonder what Germany will be like. I wonder about my girl, and how her year is going.

Chapter 10: 1965 – Just Like Old Times
Karen

It's a beautiful fall day in St. Paul, Minnesota. The leaves on the trees are bright with various colors, and the leaves that have fallen have turned brown and dry. I listen to them crunch under my feet as I walk home. I don't have any plans, tonight. I think I might just relax with a book, or maybe even just listen to the radio.

When I get to my apartment, I shed my coat and thumb through the mail. Nothing special today. I look to see if my roommate is around, and it doesn't seem that she is home yet. I walk into the kitchen and am debating if I should have a snack or try to make something for dinner when I hear a knock at the door. I open the door, and I feel my heart skip a beat. The tall handsome man in front of me is Dennis. I stand there in shock.

I don't know how he found me, but I am happy to see him. "How did you find me?" I ask.

"You do have friends, Karen. There are also phone books, which are great when you want to look up someone's address." He laughs and smiles his big, broad smile. "I wanted to see you and to see how life has been treating you."

I stare at him and then smile back. "Well, come in. Let me take your jacket. We can sit here in the living room. Can I get you anything to drink?" I ask. I am fluttering; I'm slightly nervous to see him again, but it is a good feeling of shared memories.

The next couple of hours fly by as we share stories. I tell him about life at college, and he tells me about his experiences in the Army while he was stationed in Germany. We talk about our daughter and reminisce about all the fun we had when we were younger. It seems like old times being together again.

Dinner is brought up in our conversation. I'm not hungry, but we do discuss going out for dinner. I really don't feel like going out, so I invite Dennis to stay in the apartment and have dinner with me instead of going to a restaurant. My roommate still isn't home, and it is very relaxing just chatting. I fix something simple and light to eat. We sit together on the floor of the apartment, and share a wonderful dinner. I don't want the evening to end.

"Karen, I have really enjoyed our evening. It was so good to see you and chat about the old days. It was even good to talk about our daughter. I would really like to see you again," he says with a touching smile as the evening ends.

"I would like that too, Dennis," I answer. Then I stand on my tip-toes and kiss him goodnight. As he turns around to look at me one last time before he leaves, he has a big grin on his face, and it warms my heart. *I have missed that grin!*

The next thing I know, it's Christmas, and Dennis and I are enjoying the lights that are twinkling on the Christmas tree. There is a recording of music boxes playing Christmas carols on the record player.

Dennis and I are enjoying this Christmas—being together, shopping, walking through the decorated streets, and listening to all the good Christmas music on the radio.

One evening, while we are sitting on the sofa looking through a magazine together, I reach over Dennis to change the station on the radio. We have just finished listening to "The Man with All the Toys" by the Beach Boys, and the station has gone into some commercials. I am in the mood for another Christmas song, so I want to change the station. A commercial for the Dayton's department store in downtown Minneapolis comes on the air.

Dennis grabs my hand. "Wait," he says, "I want to hear what Dayton's has for specials and sales this weekend. I still have shopping to do." He turns his head to look at me with his ever-wonderful grin.

I smile back at him, because I can't help it, and stop my hand in mid-air before turning the station. "Okay, I will leave the radio on its current station just so you can listen to what's on sale." I sit back on the sofa with a small smile on my face. This really is pleasant—just sitting, relaxing, and listening to music with Dennis. It makes me feel like it could really be an everyday part of our life.

"Honey," he says as he looks at me, "Dayton's has sales on all their men's and women's sweaters. Let's go shopping and see what we can find for my mother—and maybe even . . . you." As he says it, his tone gets more and more jovial and teasing.

I respond, "Of course you want to go to Dayton's; it's your favorite store. You want to go more for yourself than for Christmas presents." I can't help but giggle. He is the best dressed man I have ever met.

There is a small bowl of nuts on the coffee table in front of our sofa. He leans forward, grabs a couple of peanuts, and tosses them at me as he grins over his shoulder. "Give me a break, girlfriend," he says. "I really do have Christmas shopping to do."

I giggle back and quickly reply, "Okay, when is the sale—and when do you want to go?" I had only half listened to the advertisement, since I was enjoying our moment more than listening to the chatter.

"The sale is only on Saturday and Sunday this week. Let's go on a shopping date. I will pick you up in the morning; we can go shopping; and then I will take you to Donaldson's North Shore Grill for a lake trout lunch. Sound good? Can you go?" he asks excitedly.

"I will check my calendar and appointments, Mr. Vinar," I tease.

I get up off the sofa, walk over to the calendar hanging on the wall, and look at Saturday. I don't have anything planned. I didn't think I did—but it always pays to check just to make sure. I walk over to the sofa and wrap my arms around his neck and lean over to whisper in his ear, "I am free as a bird on Saturday. Let's go on that date you were just talking about." I stand up to look at him, and he has a big wide smile on his face, which causes me to lean over and go for an even bigger kiss. I can't help myself.

I wake up eager. I am excited for the day. It promises to be a bright, sunny day that will make the snow on the ground sparkle like tiny diamonds. Dennis is supposed to arrive in forty-five minutes, but I am sure he will be here in a half hour, because he always says: "If you are on time, you are late!" Unfortunately, that means that I am running late because I still have to style my hair before he gets here.

Thirty minutes later, like clockwork, a knock comes at the door, and I run to greet him. "Are you ready?" he says as I open up the door.

"Of course," I respond with a smile.

"Then hop into your chariot, madame, and let's take off on a Christmas date," he says, beaming.

I lock the apartment door and run down the sidewalk to the car where he is patiently standing, holding the car door open for me. Dennis is such a gentleman. I love that about him. Our ride into downtown Minneapolis is quick as the roads are clear and traffic is rather light on our lovely, bright Saturday morning.

We park the car in a parking ramp next to Dayton's and walk into the festive holiday atmosphere of a shopping dream. There is Christmas music playing in the background, and the sounds of "O Holy Night" meet us as we enter the front of the store, which is where the perfume department is located.

There are three Christmas trees of varying sizes that greet us. The smell of pine wafts into our nostrils, and our eyes behold the beautiful sight. The freshly cut trees are all decked out with red and gold ball ornaments, red and white lights, and gold-painted pine cones nestled amid the branches along with fancy red and white velvet bows. The branches are draped with gold tinsel giving them a very elegant look. The trees are beautiful.

To the right of the big revolving door on Nicollet Avenue, there are window displays of mannequins dressed in furs and holiday dresses— and even one window display for the kids showing Santa getting a beard trim in the barbershop. Dennis grabs my hand and holds it as we walk through the different departments. We pass the women's sweaters, and I immediately think of the yellow sweater Dennis gave me six years earlier.

"Do you still wear that sweater, hon?" Dennis asks.

"How did you know I was thinking of that?" I retort quickly with a grin.

"Your face and your eyes turned soft. I just assumed, since I caught your eyes looking at the sweaters, that you might have thought of the first gift I gave you," he says with a quick grin. I really love his grin!

I laugh then and say, "Yes, dear, I still wear it—and I still love it. I knew the moment I opened the gift years ago that it would always be a special sweater. It's perfect for our Minnesota winters when it's really cold outside."

We end up browsing in the jewelry department. He holds my hand and looks at earrings and necklaces, and then he stops at the rings. His hand tightens on mine, and I hear him softly say, "Someday, Karen Lehmann, there will be a ring on your finger." But when I look at his face, instead of a joking smile he is serious—only his eyes hold a twinkle.

We continue our relationship for several months until one night in early March. We are just coming back from a movie and are discussing my busy week of studying for finals before spending spring break visiting my family and moving to a new apartment for the rest of my junior year of college.

When Dennis comes inside to say goodnight, he softly takes hold of my shoulders and turns me so that I am facing him. He looks into my eyes and says, "Karen, will you please marry me?"

Did I hear him correctly? Without hesitation, I excitedly say "Yes," and am immediately delighted with the anticipation of planning a wedding. I feel we will be happy together. It seems like the right thing to do—except for the fact that I have always wanted to finish my college education and have a career as an interior designer.

The next weekend I drive home to Brownton to speak with my parents, excited to tell them the news.

"Mom, Dad!" I call as I open the door of the house. Um, something smells good.

"Well, hello, dear," my mother says to me as I kiss her on the cheek.

"What smells so good in here?" I ask, even though I already know.

"Oh, Grandma is baking some of her bread, and you know the house always smells good when she bakes," Mom says.

"I forgot how good it smells. I think I have been away from home too long," I say with a laugh. "Mom, I have some wonderful news," I announce.

"Oh, do you want me to call your dad into the kitchen?" she asks.

"No, let's just go into the living room and tell him."

When we get into the living room, I sit down on the sofa facing my father in his chair. I look at both of my parents and say, "Guess what? . . . Dennis asked me to marry him, and I said yes." I can tell that I have a huge grin on my face. "I am so excited. I have missed him, and in these last few months we have been dating, we have gotten even closer. I just wanted to let you know my good news."

To my dismay, they are totally against me marrying him.

"Karen, absolutely not. You are not going to marry that man," my father says with a frown.

"Dad, we are in love. We have been in love. Give me a reason why I shouldn't marry him," I cry out to him with frustration in my voice.

"Karen, I cannot agree to this marriage. I will not pay any more of your college tuition if you decide to go through with this wedding. I know you will not finish your senior year of college if you get married. I want you to finish your college education. You have come this far and are so close to graduating with a degree. I want that for you. I am sorry if this hurts you, but that is my final decision. No more dollars spent on college. End of discussion," he says with determination—and a glance at my mother.

I am heartbroken. I can feel the frustration in my heart; it is the same frustration I felt a few years earlier. Carrying a heavy heart, I go about the day with my parents and, late in the afternoon, I go back to St. Paul. I know that my friends were planning to get together at a local neighborhood spot for a burger, and I feel that I need to be with them. My roommates will be there, and I know they will help me have a good time.

Even with my friends around me, throughout the evening I can hear my father's voice. I am conflicted. I want to be with Dennis. I know he has my heart. It is very clear that I love him. My heart knows things my head doesn't. But there are things my father said that resonate with me, too. I do want a college degree. I have been focused on the outcome of the coming year so that I can do what I want for a career. I can see myself as a designer, and I can feel myself gravitating toward doing what my father wishes. But, while my head is focusing, my heart is breaking. How do I go about this? I ask myself. How do I love, but choose to take a different road?

Since my parents are convinced I will not finish school if we get married—and they refuse to pay any more college tuition if I marry Dennis—I make the decision to decline his proposal.

It is hard the day I tell him, and I can tell by the look on his face that he is both hurt and angry. I have no idea that I will live to regret my decision some day.

(Later, I will find out that Dennis would move on from me and marry another woman. Even so, in hindsight, I think together we could have convinced my parents to allow us to marry—and that we would have made the marriage work because we really loved each other.)

Chapter 11: 1966 – Struck Out Again
Dennis

When I got out of the military in September of 1965, I was 22 and Karen was 20. We got together and dated for six months. I then asked Karen to marry me again. Her immediate answer was "Yes, definitely." However, after telling her parents about our marriage plans, she changed her mind and said no, stating that she wanted a career. I was heartbroken when she said, "My father said if I marry you, he will not pay for my senior year of college."

This turn of events is not what I had in mind when I started dating Karen again. I am in love with this woman. She means the world to me. When she turned me down again, my heart broke. I am disappointed. Her father is worried about money, but I have money saved up! Even though I am still sending money to Karen's father for the birth of Denise, I have enough money saved from my tour of duty in the Army to pay for Karen's senior year of college. I know she wants a career, and I am fine with that. She can have a career. I would just like to be a part of her life.

Karen and I are finished. When she told me she wanted a career instead of a marriage, I decided that we were going nowhere as a couple. It's time to move on in life. We are moving in separate directions, and I need to start making some decisions for myself. I have some money saved up, and I think I am going to have some fun with it. *A car would be the perfect break-up gift!* I smile at the thought.

Today I am on my way to a car dealership. My desire is for some wheels that are "cool." I want a new car, and I can pay cash. I am determined to move on from our broken relationship.

As I walk in through the glass doors of the dealership, I already know the car I want. "Hello, Dad," I say, "I have my eye on the Mustang on the sales lot. What can you tell me about it?"

"Ah, she is a beauty, isn't she?" he replies. "She's got a V-8 engine, four-speed transmission, and styled wheels; and she drives smooth as silk." He goes on to detail the car's more-than-satisfactory specs. I have already made up my mind that I am going to buy it, even before he starts singing the car's praises, but he doesn't know that. Dad wants to tell me what he can about the Mustang, though, so he also explains to me that the previous owner of the Mustang committed suicide by pulling into his garage and keeping the car running as he sat inside.

After he tells me that, I say with a smile of satisfaction, "What do I care? Great. Thank you, Dad. You have just sold yourself a car."

Dad grins from ear to ear when I tell him I want to buy the Mustang. His grin gets even bigger when I pay him cash. That feels pretty good. I'm still feeling bruised after a broken relationship, but I can feel the healing begin when I am driving out of the car lot in a baby blue 1966 Ford Mustang.

As I drive around the streets of Minneapolis, I let the car take over my thoughts. When Karen told me "no" after we had been seeing each other for six months, we each went our separate ways. That's what she and her parents wanted. But it is still hard for me to accept. I know there will be other men who will love her, but I don't know whether they will love her as much as I did.

(Little did I know that I would marry another woman but it wouldn't last—and how much I would enjoy our three wonderful children. Karen would move on, as well, graduate from college, marry someone else—who will die in 2010—and be blessed with a son. But I was certain that Karen would always have a part of my heart.

Looking back, if I could do it over again, I would have gone to Brownton and talked to her parents about getting married. I would have shown them my savings account that could have paid for her senior year of college, instead of my Mustang.)

Chapter 12: 1971 – Birthday, August 13th
Dennis

The phone rings, and I immediately pick up the receiver. "Hello," I say rather brusquely and quickly, having been interrupted while my thoughts were focused on a work-related business transaction.

"Do you remember what day this is?" the caller says without any kind of greeting or introduction. It is Denise DeeAnn's tenth birthday today—and the caller is my sister reminding me once again of the child I had to give up.

"Hello," I respond with a smile at my sister's voice. "Yes, I do remember what day it is today. It is my first daughter's tenth birthday."

We have a quick conversation because we are both pretty busy. I set the receiver back on the phone, and my mind drifts off to my siblings and family members who don't let me forget. They, too, remember what I went through years ago, and I am fortunate to be surrounded by people who care. I smile at the thought.

Remembering ten years earlier, I'm reminded that holding my baby and having to give her over to the nurse who came into Karen's room was one of the toughest things I have had to do. Leaving Karen that day after I signed the birth certificate was also incredibly hard. I didn't want to leave. I wanted to stay and hold her hand and talk like we used to do.

Thinking of those days ten years ago reminds me of the girl who said "no"—and the daughter who is with someone else. I think about what our ten-year-old girl might be like. I wonder what she looks like. I wonder if she is in good care.

Looking around my office, I take note that it's small but comfortable. The phone is where most of my business is conducted. The surface of my desk has a couple stacks of paper, but for the most part it is clean. I don't like a lot of clutter. There is a framed photo of my wife, four-year-old daughter, and me that was taken last year. I smile when I look at it.

As I reminisce, I think of my four-year-old daughter, who is a little sweetheart. She is the girl who is with me and running around being an adorable four-year-old. She is home with me. I get to be with her every day, and that thought brings another smile. I wonder what she will be like when she is ten.

The phone rings, once more interrupting my thoughts. This time it is a business call. I am back on track, and all thoughts of the past and present are left behind. My mind is back on my work.

Chapter 13: 1971 – The Lie

Jean

10 years old, 5th grade

"Jean, get in the kitchen and do those dishes! NOW!" yells my dad from the basement, where he often sequesters himself amongst the piles of papers he has stacked on his big wooden desk. At ten years old, I hear him and know I have to do the dishes, but I am immersed in a TV show—my *favorite* TV show—that I watch on our twenty-five-inch Zenith color TV set. David Cassidy is on the screen, and I am wishing so desperately that I was a sister in the Partridge family. As I rock in my dad's big, brown, over-stuffed rocking chair, I feel like I want to be in their family in the worst way. I am obsessed by it. Every morning when I walk down the driveway to school I actually talk out loud to David Cassidy—my imaginary big brother.

Dad yells at me again.

"Daddy, can I just have ten more minutes? Then I will go wash the dishes. I promise," I call back to him.

I don't hear any sounds coming from the basement. I look at the big clock hanging on the wall, and realize that my show will soon be over—and I will be alone again. The Partridge Family will not be around to keep me company. I know Dad won't come up for a while, and, when he does, he will turn the TV to a station or show that he wants to watch. As long as he hears me rustling around in the kitchen—and the dishes are done when he comes upstairs—everything will be fine.

When the show is over and I hear the last notes of the song playing over the ending credits, I feel gloomy. I walk to the kitchen and fill

61

the dishwasher with all the dinner dishes. Our big, old clumsy dishwasher is a pain. Even so, I know dishwashers are the latest thing to help mothers in the kitchen—and in some ways I am happy I don't have to wash every single dish. Then I notice the broiler pan. Gosh, Mom had another hamburger before she went to work tonight. I have to wash the stupid broiler pan again. I can't put that in this dishwasher. I hate washing the broiler pan. I can't stand it. It truly makes me mad.

I bet Mrs. Partridge doesn't eat hamburgers every day, and I bet she doesn't make Laurie wash the broiler pan even if she does make hamburgers. What would it be like to have a big sister? She could do all the dishes, I think. What would it be like to have a little sister like Tracy? I bet she is fun to play with. I wish I had sisters. I really wish that I had Keith as a brother. I could be in the family band. Tracy and I could play tambourine together. I could sing with Keith! I could have a mom who wouldn't make hamburgers for every meal. I scrub the broiler pan and get it as clean as I can. I hate that thing! Then I start the dishwasher.

Tonight I am yawning. I had a good day at school, but I have to do more homework, and I don't like the story the teacher is making us read. I like happy stories, not these sad ones. I really don't want to read this book at all. It's called The Secret Garden. My teacher says it's about a girl whose mother and father die and she has to go live with her uncle in England. That just makes me sad. The uncle is probably mean. The teacher says I should give it a chance. Well . . . I had better go read the first chapter, but I feel like I just want to sleep.

I crawl into my bed with the book. I love my big double bed. It's huge and very comfy with two big, fluffy pillows, and two thick, heavy, colorful patchwork quilts that my grandma made me. I get comfortable with the pillows fluffed behind me and start reading. I knew it. It's sad. I already don't like it. I close my eyes, and all I can see in my mind is Keith Partridge. He is helping me with my homework. He is telling me that he will read the book for me and tell me what I need to know for the test. I am so happy.

The weekend went by in a blur, and I didn't pick up that book the teacher wanted us to read. Oh gosh, it's already Monday morning. I must have fallen asleep last night while reading my book. My mom has just called me to get up for school. My book is lying on my dresser.

Mom comes into my room and smiles at me. I love seeing my mom in the morning. She always wakes me up with a smile. My mom is the best. She is really nice, and she loves to chat with me in the mornings when I am getting ready for school.

"I see you are reading a book for school. I think you will like this one, Jean; it's a good one about the hard work that goes into a special garden," she says in this really happy, positive tone. My mom loves her garden—of course, she would say that.

"Mom, the first chapter is horrible. The poor girl's mom dies. I don't want to read a book about a girl whose mom dies," I complain. I look at her like she is crazy . . . Ugh.

"Oh, give it a chance. I've read this one. It gets better. You will like it—trust me. I made you some pancakes this morning for breakfast. Come into the kitchen and have some before you brush your teeth," she says cheerfully. Then she kisses my cheek. "You should have started reading it on Friday night, Jean. You shouldn't have left it until Sunday," she adds as she walks to the kitchen.

Ooh, pancakes. My favorite breakfast. I hurry to get dressed, brush my hair, and then run to the kitchen. It smells so good. I wolf down the pancakes, grab my school things, and race out the door for school. I get on the school bus, and there is an open seat in front of my friend Sheila.

"Hi, Sheila, did you watch it Friday night?" I ask as soon as I plop down on the seat.

"Yes! It was wonderful. I love David Cassidy. He is so cute. I want him as a boyfriend," she declares with puppy love. "Did you like the song they sang, Jean?"

"I always like the songs they sing. I should learn how to play the guitar. Then I could be a part of their band. Do you think my mom would allow me to have guitar lessons?"

Sheila looks at me with exasperation, "Jean, they are a family. You can't just join their band. You have to be a member of the family. Besides, you don't even have a guitar."

We talk a little bit about the show, and then another friend comes on the bus and sits with Sheila. They start talking about something else, I think it was a dog, but I didn't pay attention to their conversation anymore.

I think about what Sheila said. I hadn't thought of Keith Partridge as a boyfriend. I turn up my nose at the thought. I just want him for a brother. I miss my own little brother. My brother is deaf, and he goes to a different school than I do. We don't get to see each other very much during the school year. He only comes home for long weekends once in a while. It makes me sad to think about it, because he comes home for the summer, and it is so fun to have someone with whom to play.

This summer we had such a good time together. The whole family even went on vacation to a resort called Bowstring in northern Minnesota. The resort is on Bowstring Lake, and my brother and I caught some fish! I caught a crappie right off the dock. We got to go swimming in the pool, too. We had such fun, and now I miss him. He went back to school two weeks ago. My mom cries when he goes back to school. When I see her cry, I cry, too. I think he gets to come home in October. I will like that a lot. That will make Mom happy, too.

Suddenly, a thought comes into my head: David Cassidy could be my brother. I know he could be. I don't know anything about who I really am. Nobody does. I am adopted. My mom doesn't even know who my brother would be. My dad doesn't know—if Daddy knew, he would tell me. I know he would.

The day slowly drones on, and later, in my fifth-grade classroom, we are discussing the book we were supposed to read over the weekend. We were expected to read the first chapter, and I didn't get all the way through it. I had started to read it when I got into bed but there were some very big words that I wasn't sure about and I just didn't like it. In class, I paid some attention as the teacher talked a little bit about what was happening in the first chapter. What got my full attention is when my teacher said the girl, Mary, was spoiled. *Spoiled? Really? I didn't think that Mary was spoiled.* All I thought about was that her mom died. That would be awful! Who would want to read a story about a mom dying?

The rest of September passes by quickly for me, and soon it is time for my brother, William, to come home for a long weekend. Because

William is deaf, he goes to a special school in Faribault called the W. Roby Allen School for the Deaf.

We live in the country. It's a beautiful place. The fall leaves crunch under my shoes, and everything is colorful. I sometimes just wish I wasn't alone so much. I know William is my little brother, but I don't always think of him as younger, even though he is only seven-and-a-half years old.

Since it's October, a lot of leaves have fallen from our big trees down by the creek. William and I have a favorite tree. You know, actually, it looks like it is kind of three trees that have merged together. It's kind of weird to look at. The trunks of the trees are all together at the base and they don't stand tall, they kind of lean in different directions. William and I really like it. We have a fort in the middle of those trees. We can put our feet in there, and this weekend we took a whole bunch of leaves and a little bit of mud for packing and we kind of made a floor for our fort. We can stand in it, or even sit in the bottom of it, now that we have put all those leaves in there.

We spent the whole weekend fooling around outside with leaves and our fort at the creek. When Sunday came around and it was time for him to go back to school, I said to him, "I don't want you to go. I need you here with me. Can't you go to school here?"

William is really smart. He has learned to lip read. So I talk slow and make him look at me, which is how we can talk to one another. He always says it's easy to read my lips. That makes me happy.

He understands exactly what I've said. He nods his head and says he wishes he could be home with me. "I miss you too, Jean. Christmas is coming, I will get to see you then," he says.

He cries when we leave him at the school, and so do Mom and I.

Monday, the day after we dropped William off at school, I am on the bus talking to Sheila.

She says, "Are you going to watch it this week, Jean?"

"If my dad lets me, am I going to watch our favorite show?" I say back to her with a big grin and a little giggle. Just thinking about The Partridge Family makes me smile and get excited.

"Friday night is the last football game of the season. Is your dad going to make you go to the game with him? If you have to go, then you won't get to watch TV. I know I don't have to go to the football game with my parents. I am so excited—I get to watch it!" she declares.

I think about this. She's right; it is the last football game of the season. Dad is going to make me go with him. I know it. He will never let me stay home by myself. Maybe next year he will let me stay home alone if he wants to go to a football game. He thinks there are a couple of senior boys that could play college ball because they are so good. I suddenly get mad. If this is the last home game, I won't be enjoying The Partridge Family; I will be freezing at the sidelines of a football game listening to Dad laugh and chat with his friends.

Sheila sees me wrinkle up my nose and says, "Don't worry. I will fill you in with all the details on Monday." I can feel myself get crabby.

The teacher looks right at me a few hours later in our reading class. Our class is almost half way through the book, along with our other reading assignments from our reading book. I have been keeping up with the chapters lately because I do like the book—I won't tell my mom though. I don't want to admit to her that she was right and now I like the book. The teacher asks, "Jean, can you tell me how you felt in this chapter when Mary first met Colin?"

"I want to find a brother like Colin in my house," I blurt out without thinking.

All the kids laugh. The teacher looks around the room and says, "We all would like to find new playmates, wouldn't we?"

Then the kids all start wanting to tell their own stories, and I sink low into my chair with a red face and a feeling like I want to cry. I can't cry. Don't cry right now, I tell myself. But I feel a little tear in the corner of my eye, and I angrily swipe at it. I catch my teacher's eye, and she gives me a wink. Oh, good, she isn't mad at me. I thought she was going to yell at me for saying something stupid.

I think about *The Secret Garden* and daydream a little about finding David Cassidy in the basement of my house sitting on a chair and strumming a guitar. Oh, how I would love to find a big brother in the basement. Even as I daydream, I know it is impossible, but an idea just keeps popping into my head. An idea that maybe I could feel better about everything if I just told a story.

I climb the two steps into the school bus, and Sheila is sitting by herself. I sit down beside her.

"Guess what?" I say to her with a smile.

"What?" She asks.

"I got a special phone call today! I am so excited," I announce.

"Who called you? Why are you so excited? Why did they call you at school? Did you have to go to the office?" she asks.

"Yes," I say rather importantly, "I did have to go to the office and talk to the principal. He was on the phone with David Cassidy!" I lied in an excited whisper.

"What?" she exclaims, "Oh, Jean, you are lying! What a liar. Why would you say something like that?"

I look at her and calmly, with a straight face, say, "I am not lying." I cross my heart. "Cross my heart and hope to die, stick a needle in my eye, I am telling the truth. David Cassidy called the principal."

"Well, I don't believe you. Why would David Cassidy call the principal?" she asks.

I answer her back in a whisper, "I just found out that I am David Cassidy's sister."

She totally laughs out loud and says, "That is the biggest lie I have ever heard. Why would you tell me, your best friend, a lie like that?"

"Sheila, I am adopted. I have known for a long time that my mom and dad picked me out of a group of babies. I don't know my real parents or my real brothers. But I just found out that David Cassidy is my brother. Don't tell anyone. David is such a big star that he doesn't want anyone to know about me. So it's just a secret between you and me. Okay?"

She looks at me funny. I am ready to tell her that I am kidding when she says, "Oh my goodness. You are David Cassidy's sister? I am so jealous. That is so cool. Do you think you will ever get to meet him?"

"I am not sure, Sheila. I am not sure of anything. I just know that I got to talk to him a little bit on the phone in the principal's office, and he said that he wanted to tell me hi," I lie.

"Ooohhh," she breathlessly says. "That is so cool, Jean."

"I have to go to the football game with my dad on Friday night, so I won't get to watch The Partridge Family, but David said he will call me on Saturday and let me know what the episode is all about," I say as I continue on the lying streak.

I really was going to tell her that I was just joking, but she ended up believing me. I thought that was really funny. In fact, I laugh out loud at the thought when I get off the bus. I laugh all the way into the house. Some kids are so gullible.

The next Monday morning I get on the bus, and Sheila pats the seat she is sitting in. "Here, I saved this spot for you. You have to tell me if you talked to David on Saturday. Did he tell you all about the episode?" she asks, animatedly whispering.

When she asks the question, for a minute I look at her and think, What is she talking about? And then I remember the lie I had told last Monday. Then I remember the lie I told on Tuesday. Then I remember how mad I got on Friday when I had to go to the stupid football game. I smile at her and say, "No. He didn't call." I was about ready to tell her that it was all a joke, but then something snapped inside me. I am not sure why I did it, but I told her that David Cassidy might come to visit me.

That was a mistake.

She was full of questions. "Why does he want to come and visit you now? Can he get away from the TV show? Is he going to bring anyone with him? Who is David's mother? If he is your brother, is his mother your mother?"

I sit and quietly ponder all of these questions and really am thinking I should fess up about it being a joke when, instead, I say, "He misses me, Sheila. He says he wants to meet his sister who he just found out about. I don't know who my mom is, but he said he will tell me all about it when he comes to Minnesota to meet me."

She looks at me with her big blue eyes and says, "I want to meet him too, Jean. Can you introduce me to him? Please? Please?"

"Of course, Sheila. I will tell him when I talk to him that you want to meet him," I lie again.

This was a big mistake. As the week goes by, I tell even more lies and begin to feel kind of bad about it. I am not sure how to get out of the big fat lie I have told.

To make it even worse, Sheila blabs. She can't keep her mouth shut. She tells her brother. And then her brother tells their sister, who is a freshman in high school.

Her sister corners me in front of the bus and says to me, "If David Cassidy is your brother, and my sister gets to meet him, I get to meet him too. I have a letter I want to give to him. And, I am going to ask him to meet my friends!" She glares at me, and then she says, "You better not be lying, you little brat! If you are, you are going to pay for that lie."

Yep—I am scared. I feel like crawling in a hole. *Oh my goodness. I am going to be killed by Sheila's sister, the big brute of the bus. Yikes!*

The next Friday, after I had been telling another week of lies that I couldn't help, my mom meets me at the door when I come home from school.

"Jean Marie, I have some questions for you," she says in an angry voice.

Uh-oh . . . what did I do now? I ask myself.

"I got a phone call today from Sheila's mother. She told me that you have been telling a rumor. There is no point in you lying to me right now. I do have the facts, but I want you to tell me exactly what you have been saying," she glares at me when she speaks. She is mad.

I feel bad. I want the floor to swallow me whole. "I told Sheila that David Cassidy was my brother," I say in a very meek and weak voice.

"That is what Sheila's mother told me on the phone. How in the world could you tell a lie like that? Haven't you been listening in Sunday school about telling lies and how things can get out of control when you lie like that?" she asks. Then she looks at me and says, "I am very disappointed in you, Jean. It breaks my heart that you could weave such an elaborate lie. Go get the hair brush. You will be punished and disciplined for such an awful thing."

Mother spanked me then, and, of course, I cried. I am more hurt by her disappointment in me than by the hair brush, though. I just feel really bad. I don't talk too much the whole weekend. I stay away from my parents. I walk down by the creek and sit in my tree. I sit in the leaves and mud (and more leaves) that William and I had put in the middle of the trees as a floor just a few weeks earlier. I sit in my tree and cry a little and think about a lot of things.

I think about what I said and the lie I told, and I feel bad. I also think about my parents and how I sometimes feel so alone. I still daydream about what it would be like to be David Cassidy's sister—even though that is what got me into trouble in the first place. I just can't stop my mind from daydreaming about it. I daydream about a house full of laughter, of singing songs, of traveling around the country in a colorful painted school bus with my mom as the driver, and of just a bunch of happiness.

It is getting colder, and I know snow is coming. This awful weekend I punish myself by making myself stay outside in the cold. I try to stay warm by walking and kicking leaves, but I am angry with myself, feel sorry for myself, and miss my brother. I don't get to watch any TV the whole weekend, and my mom says I have to read the whole book of The Secret Garden for school, even though my teacher didn't say we had to finish it. Mom even asks me questions on Sunday night about the book. I know she is using the book as a punishment, but in reality I have immersed myself in The Secret Garden.

The book I am reading for school has become one of my favorites now. I didn't think I was going to like it at all and now that I have read it, I want to read it again. I even like Mary, and sometimes I feel like I would love to lie in my bed and talk to her. It would be so nice to have a sister like her. When Dickon brought the lamb into Colin's bedroom, I thought of feeding the baby kittens in my Grandpa Carl's barn. I like it when Grandpa takes the cow's teat and streams warm milk into the cats' mouths. I think of this and giggle when I read about Colin feeding the baby lamb.

I can see Mary and Dickon in the garden working with the crocuses (I had to go to the dictionary and look up that word, along with other plants that were mentioned in the book) and pulling weeds like I have to do in the summer with my mom in our garden. I am rereading my favorite parts of the book on Sunday night when my mom comes into my bedroom and sits on the bed next to me. She reaches over and tenderly sweeps the hair out of my face.

"Jean, why? Why did you tell Sheila that lie?" Mom asks me.

I think about the question for a while and say to the floor, making sure I don't meet my mom's eyes, "I don't want to be alone all the time. I want William home. I want a sister to play with. I want a brother to do things with. I don't know anyone who is all alone. None of my friends are alone except Archer. . . . I don't think he has any sisters or brothers, but he lives too far away from me to ever want to play with me."

"I am here," she says. "So is your dad. You aren't alone."

"I don't have anyone to play with. You work a lot at night, and Dad goes into his office or is watching TV shows," I say looking down. "I feel lonely."

"Oh, that is ridiculous," she says rather hurriedly and almost sounding annoyed. "You are never alone. Even if your dad and I are busy, you should always be able to find something to do. Do your homework. Clean your room. You could clean it every day. Read more books. Play with your dolls. There are plenty of things to do to keep you occupied so that you don't feel bored," she says dismissively as she walks away.

I am alone again with those parting words from Mom. I never said anything to her about being bored. I hardly ever am bored. I am happy entertaining myself; I just want to be with someone else. I don't always like to play by myself. I have two friends who are twins who live up the gravel road. Dad says it's only about a half-mile to walk to their house, but I don't get to walk there on my own. I think about them now and I get jealous just thinking about it. They always have each other, plus they have other sisters and brothers. I love visiting them when my mom allows me to ride my bike to their house. I wouldn't mind having a twin. I would love to have a twin with me right now.

I start to cry again because I am even lonelier now than I was before. I close my eyes and fall asleep thinking of Dickon, Mary, and Colin—and how they found each other. And about how they worked to turn a secret garden full of dead twigs, branches, leaves, and weeds into a place of beauty with color and life. I can see the garden in my mind—full of pink and yellow roses and purple . . . whatever those other flowers are called. I see the daisies and the green ferns and the big swing on the oak tree. I love their camaraderie and companionship.

Mary had been all alone, but now she has Dickon, Colin, and even her uncle as he learns about the work they all have done to transform the garden. At the end of the book, Mary's uncle chooses to be with them to work and to play in the garden. I fall asleep with tears drying my eyelashes shut.

I fall asleep feeling sad . . . because I don't want to be alone anymore. I want Mary, Dickon, and Colin in my life—not just in a book. I want David Cassidy and all of the Partridge family as my own family because I don't want to be alone any more.

I want my brother home with me because I don't want to be alone any more.

Chapter 14: 1978 through the late-1980s – Life Goes On

Karen

My goal of finishing college in four years was accomplished in June of 1967. My first job—selling furniture, flooring, and window coverings—lasted only three years, ending when the owner of the store retired. Even so, I was encouraged to proceed with my chosen profession and quickly found another position in an interior design studio, all the while saving money to buy a home.

Working took priority over dating, and I soon succeeded in becoming a homeowner—with the responsibilities that go along with maintaining a house and yard. Moving into my own little house (that I could paint any color I wished instead of being trapped in "apartment white" walls) was thrilling to me as I stripped layers of wallpaper off the walls and "peel-n-stick" floor tiles off the floor. I unpacked boxes and hung pictures until I had everything just the way I wanted it.

In the process of unpacking things that have been stored away for a while as I moved from apartment to apartment, I just came across a baby picture with a little card that reads: "August 13, 1961." This is the first picture taken of Denise. I remember that Sunday. She was born on that day at 10:35 AM. The photo also lists her length of twenty inches and her weight of seven pounds, nine ounces. This is the only photo of my daughter that I have. She looks so much like her father, Dennis.

Dennis and I have lost touch with each other except for one night earlier this year when Dennis once again appeared at my door without warning. Again we reminisced about our past times together, but this time he spoke excitedly about his business as a manufacturer's rep—as well as his beautiful daughter and his wife. I believe he said that he was living in Wisconsin, but unfortunately I didn't get his contact information.

After that unexpected visit, once again, we did not talk for several years.

I eventually married a realtor, and we started a design-build company in St. Paul. When I found out I was pregnant again, it brought back memories of my first pregnancy and my daughter. I kept comparing the feelings I had during the two pregnancies and wondered frequently what happened to the daughter I gave up for adoption.

When I gave birth to my son and first took him to daycare, I would look at all of the sweet faces of the children there and wonder what color hair and eyes Denise had. By the time I had my son, Denise would have been in her mid-twenties. So many unanswered questions kept popping up in my mind: *Did she go to college? Did she get married? Does she have children of her own? Where does she live? Is she even alive?*

My son grew up as an only child. I often wondered how he would have gotten along with a sibling if I had had another baby. My career was important to me, though, which is one of the reasons I did not marry until age thirty-five. Having a baby at forty years old was risky, but the decision was made after my husband and I weighed the pros and cons together. Our son was a blessing, and I don't regret my decision. Spending time with him while he grew up was a joy. I was the proud parent, watching him pitch at his baseball games and eagerly cheering for him.

Sometime in the late 1980s Dennis calls me on the phone inviting me to have lunch. It is an invitation which I eagerly accept. He is apologetic in his conversation, wanting to make amends for any harm he may have caused me. I will find out, later, that he had gone through treatment for alcoholism, and this was all a part of his program.

Sometime after that, I even seek out his help and information on alcoholism at a time when I think my husband might be an alcoholic, as well.

Chapter 15: 1979 - A Tumultuous Year
Jean

January – Divorce

Mom and I are sitting in my car in Rochester, Minnesota, outside of the hotel she has been living in for the last month. The January cold is kept outside of the warm interior of the car, but I feel cold and alone. I am really unhappy right now and fighting to keep from crying. Mom has just told me that she and Tom are going to get married as soon as her divorce from Dad is final.

I remember my brother, William, and I talking last summer in the back yard. He said he noticed something funny about Mom. He said she was "different," but I didn't agree with him. The only thing I noticed that was vaguely different was that I didn't see Dad kiss Mom goodbye before he left for work like I had seen him do before. That was different, but I had argued with William and said everything was fine. I have since realized that deaf people have extra sensitivity with their other senses. He probably would have noticed changes in Mom and Dad more than I. He also might have noticed because he doesn't live in the house like I do. He can sense subtle changes that I don't see since I'm there every day. This makes me sad as I think that I didn't see this coming.

Mom sat me down last October and informed me that she had asked Dad for a divorce. She had fallen for another man, Tom. This news came as a complete shock to me. "Why, Mom?" I had asked. I remember being in shock at first, and then, a couple of days later, anger set in.

I have known Tom for a couple of years. He is a nice guy. He is the bartender at the Chanticleer Room at the Rochester airport. I have worked with him because I was the coat check girl last winter on one or two Friday or Saturday nights for the restaurant. Tom and Mom have worked together for the last two years. I guess they fell in love. In my mind, I do not understand how a person can just fall out of love with the man to whom she is married. This just doesn't make sense to me. The day she told me she was going to leave was a horrible day, and as I sit here now, I am choosing to ignore all thoughts and memories of that day.

Mom stayed with Dad, William, and me through Christmas, for the sake of my brother and me. She slept in my brother's bedroom until he came home for the holiday, and then she slept on the sofa. She tried to pretend she was enjoying Christmas, but in reality all four of us knew it was the last one we would all share together—and it was really uncomfortable. During our Christmas vacation from school, Mom made suppers for William and me (and Dad), but she hardly touched her food. Dinner table conversation for most of my life had been congenial and informational. This Christmas season it was next to nothing. Verbal exchanges were mostly between William and me. Dad would eat and ignore the giant elephant in the room. Then he would go sit down in his La-Z-Boy rocker in the living room and fall asleep watching some mindless show. Mom would clean up the supper dishes and do anything other than sit in the living room with him. She wouldn't even come into the living room if William and I were in there. It was the most "fake" Christmas I had ever experienced in all of my seventeen years.

Mom moved to the hotel the day after Christmas. I remember watching her pack her car that day. William and I watched her drive down the driveway. I sobbed and felt angry—and deserted. She is leaving me. She is leaving our family. I felt a pang of ever-present loneliness creep under my skin. I looked at my brother, and he was stoic at the moment, but I could see that he had unshed tears of his own. He turned and looked at me and said, "We can go to Rochester and see her tomorrow, Jean." Then he turned away and walked upstairs to his bedroom, and I heard the door close behind him. I was so hurt that I had a headache, and my chest felt like a weight was sitting on it.

Now it is a couple of weeks later, and she has just told me that the court date is set for January thirty-first. After that, my mother and Tom are leaving town to drive a camper all the way down to Brookport, Illinois. I don't even know where Brookport is located. She just told me that they pooled their money and bought a camper with it. A camper?

"Mom, what are you going to do with a camper?" I ask. I really can't believe this is happening to me. I am astonished by this new revelation from her.

She answers back, "We are going to live in the camper. We are driving down to Brookport where Tom's father lives. He has a few acres of land, so we talked with him, and we are going to park the camper at his place for a while until we can get enough money to get our own place."

"What about me, Mom? What am I supposed to do without you?" I ask.

She smiles at me and says, "You need to stay here and graduate from high school. You will be fine without me. You and your dad have gotten along fine in the past when I worked nights. You both will be fine. And, in time, things will get into their own routine."

"Mom, . . . I need you. I need your support. I am a senior in high school. I have four-and-a-half months left of school, and I am already behind in some of my classes. Please don't leave." I can feel the tears sting my eyes, and all of a sudden they come tumbling down my cheeks. "Mom, just let me come with you then. I can graduate down in Illinois," I cry.

She has tears of her own, but her resolve is strong. "You will be fine, Jean. It might be hard at first, but things will get better. Go to school. Work hard, and pull your grades up. Graduate and make some summer plans. You need to stay here. There isn't any room in the camper for three of us to actually live in it. When we get down to Illinois, let us get settled, and then maybe we will see if you can come and spend a couple of weeks with us in the summer. It might work out." She says the last sentence rather weakly through her own unshed tears.

I do not believe my mom. I do not believe her comforting words of coming to Illinois will come true. Thoughts are running fast and furious in my head, and I am feeling cold and alone. She is abandoning me. The word "abandoned" pops up in my head. Interesting how that word can just pop up out of nowhere. Feelings of rejection come barreling into my mind. I have felt alone so often in my young life. Rather quickly and fleetingly, an image runs through my mind of a baby in a crib in a hospital just being left there. Abandonment. From a mother who couldn't keep her child seventeen years ago, to a mother who needs to escape her life for a different one. I was left once and am being left again—by mothers. I have two mothers, and both of them have left me. I don't know anyone who feels like I do. I don't know anyone who has had the same experiences, and I don't know where to go with these feelings of loneliness and rejection. I have thought about my adoption a few times before when kids in school have peppered me with questions about being adopted. It usually does not bother me, though, because I have been happy. Maybe I have been lonely, but I have been happy. My parents truly are loving people who only want the best for me. I know this. I know they love me. I just can't stop these feelings from surfacing.

Today I feel my mom is abandoning me. I really do, and so I voice this to her. I see that by my voicing that word, I have caused her tears to fall. I do not mean to hurt her . . . but, then again, I am feeling such deep pain and hurt myself, maybe I do mean to hurt her. Maybe I wanted her to feel a little bit of what I was feeling so I said something hurtful.

June – Graduation

I can hear the high school band starting to play "Pomp and Circumstance." Sheila is in the band. She is a year younger than I am and will graduate next year. Ever since our little "David Cassidy" story happened, she has been pretty aloof. Even now, after seven years, she still seems pretty bitter about that whole incident. The only class we ever shared was band. The juniors are taking the lead role today, and the band sounds pretty good to me, but I have always loved "Pomp and Circumstance." It's an easy song to play, even for the juniors. *Haha.*

Today I am okay. It's been a rough four months, and as I look back on it, I have no idea how I got everything done in order to graduate. My senior advisor and creative writing teachers have been my advocates, and I am so grateful for their continued support. My creative writing teacher, Mrs. Simon, is great, and I am going to miss her when I go off to college. She is so positive and refreshing that it makes me wonder what college professors are like. Are they supportive, too?

I look at Doris (who is my ceremony partner for entering the gym) and say, "Here we go, Dor! It's college bound for us—I am excited to move into another chapter of life."

She grins back, then whispers, "This is insane! I can't wait to get to Stout. I wish you were going with me. You will have to come up to Stout on the weekends in the fall. We can go to football games. It will be so fun!"

"Oh, you know I will, Doris! Stout isn't that far from Rochester. We can go back and forth," I instantly respond with a mischievous grin.

The teacher is glaring at all of us graduates and yips, "Students! Get into your lines and get moving. They are waiting for you!" She is standing at the door making these big sweeping motions with her arms, trying to get all of us moving—but not too fast. She is now yipping about some kind of "mode of decorum."

Whatever, I think to myself.

Mom is here today. Just the thought of her in the gym excites me. I scan the crowd, hoping to see her as I walk into the gym with Doris. Mom flew up from Illinois, but Tom didn't come with her. It was so good to see her last weekend when I picked her up from the airport. I had missed her terribly and cried when I saw her, but they were "happy to see you" tears. As we were driving to my grandma's house in Alden, I talked a lot. There were so many things I wanted to tell her, and Mom sat with a smile on her face and listened to all of my teenage chatter. I couldn't believe how happy I was to see her and be with her. I told her I loved her at least five times on the drive from Minneapolis. She always responded with "I love you, too." Just thinking about it brings a smile to my face.

My aunt, my mom's oldest sister, had a graduation party for me last night, which was really nice of her. It was fantastic to see all of my cousins, because I have missed them, too. Last night, at my party, my cousins and I compared notes about our different summer adventures and then college plans for the fall. My cousin Patty and I are going to be in the same dorm in Rochester, and we are both excited about that. It will be so nice to have her in the same building—and I think we even are on the same floor! Thinking about all of this makes me sort of drift into my own little world as I listen to the speeches by the salutatorian and valedictorian.

Then, as the names of my classmates are read off, my thoughts shift to this afternoon and the graduation party that my dad and his sister, my Aunt Karen, have been planning. She has been so great for my dad! She asked him if she could have the party for me, and—of course—he said yes. He hasn't been very well, emotionally, since Mom left, and I think he was totally grateful that Aunt Karen volunteered to have my grad party for him.

Right after my party today, I am going to pick up my mom at Grandma's and then Mom and I are going to drive to Illinois. I am all packed. I even have my car packed already. I am really excited. She is allowing me to come down for two weeks to stay with her and Tom. She told me she wants to drive all night. I am not sure about that idea, but I am up for an adventure, and so she was able to convince me that we should get going right away.

Mom comes over to me after the graduation ceremony and swiftly hugs me. "Jean, I will see you after your party with your dad. Have fun, and we will get going as soon as you pick me up. Are you ready?" Then she spies my dad and abruptly walks away.

"Mom, where are you going?" I call after her.

She turns around, looks at me and says, "I am going back to Grandma's. I will see you later."

Gosh, can't they even look at each other? For goodness' sake, they were married for twenty years. I don't understand Mom's hasty retreat.

The "congratulation line" is winding down as Dad and my brother approach. "Are you ready to go to your party?" Dad asks. He has a smile on his face, but his eyes are not smiling. I suppose graduation is tough on every father, but I am sure he spied Mom. That probably didn't help.

My smile back to him instantly appears. He may be going through some tough stuff right now, but this last month he seemed to be a little more thoughtful. I want to reassure him that I am fine, that William is fine, and that everything will be fine. "Dad, I am ready for the party—ready to ditch Hayfield High School forever!" I laugh as I say that last line. "Come on, Daddy—let's go and have some cake!" I hook my arm in his as we walk toward the parking lot.

Parents are weird. Why did I not know they weren't getting along last summer? William knew. He pointed it out to me. How could I live in the same house as someone and not know they aren't happy? Explain this to me. I look off to the parking lot and see so many mothers, fathers, and grandparents of my classmates. I see the aunts and uncles. I see the brothers and sisters. The parking lot is a sea of people. I see one husband help his wife into the car. My dad used to do that—help my mom into the car—when I was young. I hadn't seen him help her into the car for the last few years. In fact, I don't remember the last time he helped her into the car.

I wonder what happened to my parents. Can people fall out of love? Can parents fall out of love with their own children? I notice my classmate Zack and his father walking to their car, which isn't too far away from where we are parked. As I am thinking about parents, I only see Zack's father. I don't see his mother. I wonder where she is. Zack smokes a lot of dope. (I know this is a fact; the whole school knows this fact.) It is graduation day, and Zack's hair looks as if he didn't even comb it. If I were his mother, would I fall out of love with him because of a certain behavior? Do parents fall out of love with their children? Maybe my mom fell out of love with me. Maybe I did something wrong. She left. I didn't.

"Dad?" I ask hesitantly as we walk to the car. "Mom was here. She left right away. She seemed like she didn't want to see you—or she was embarrassed to be by me."

He slows down his walk and looks at me. "I didn't expect her to want to see me, Jean. She left us. She has a different life. She didn't waste any time leaving one man and going to another. I guess if she can act so cold, so can I. I don't care to see her again."

He smiles, then says, "Hey, it isn't right to be sad today. It's your day to be happy, and I am proud of you! You are special, and you have a future ahead of you that is bright. Let's go have a good afternoon with family. It's time for celebration and cake!"

"Dad," I say tentatively, "maybe it wasn't you she wanted to leave; maybe it was me. Maybe I did something that she didn't like. Maybe I wasn't the daughter she thought I should be. Maybe she regretted getting me, adopting me."

Dad swiftly grabs my shoulders to turn me to him and fiercely, almost angrily, gives me a hug. "Don't you ever think a thing like that again!" he exclaims. "It wasn't you she wanted to leave, Jean. You know that. Don't ever think of it. Your mother still loves you, and she always will."

When I turn to look at him, his eyes are a little red. I know his heart is hurting. I can feel it by looking at his face. He never dreamed that he would be alone, without my mom, on my graduation day.

I suddenly feel tired. I heard what Dad said, but in my heart I wonder if I am right. If I were a mom, would I leave my child? Was life really that bad for her? I don't know the answer to that. That is something she has not been able to talk about with me. She has never given me good reasons for just leaving us like that. All she says is that she "didn't feel loved by Dad anymore."

My afternoon graduation party is quickly over, and I wonder where the time went. It's always so nice to be with my family, and I got such a big surprise from Dad: Grandpa Carl and Grandma Ruth are taking me to Norway with them in July! I am so shocked. I almost started to cry this afternoon when they made the announcement. Norway, *gosh* . . . I am going to Norway. I can't believe they are taking me with them. I knew Grandpa and Grandma were going to go—it's been a topic of conversation since Christmas—but I never dreamed I would get to go with them. My Aunt Karen and cousin Patricia Diane are going as well. This is so exciting, I am just astounded. I pinch my arm. *Ow, that hurts.* Okay, I guess I am not dreaming. I can't stop the huge smile from forming on my face.

After my graduation party this afternoon, I said goodbye to Dad and William. I am hoping those two will do okay without me for a couple of weeks. I picked up Mom from Grandma's house, and we got on the road quickly. Mom has it in her head that she wants to drive all night. Even though I agreed to it, now that we're driving I am still not sure I like this plan, but I don't have a choice. She has just gotten irritated with me for falling asleep. It's eleven at night, though, and we have been on the road since seven. I know that it's only been four hours, but I am so tired. It has been a long and emotional day for me. She must be tired, too, because I see her eyes drooping, and she is irritable.

"Mom, are you sure you don't want to stop and get some sleep?" I ask.

She responds with, "Yes. I just don't have enough money for a hotel room, and I guess I am tired, Jean. I didn't mean to snap at you. I was just hoping we could talk and keep each other awake."

"Maybe we should stop for some coffee at the next truck stop," I say as we enter a big construction zone full of harsh illumination for the road workers and flashing yellow warning lights for drivers. For the next few minutes we are quiet in the car as she navigates through the construction. My mind wanders, and a few minutes later I ask her, "So, Mom, what is life like with Tom? Are you happy? Are you glad you left? Do you miss Dad at all?"

She doesn't answer right away. I think she is formulating her response. She then says, "I did the right thing, Jean. I had to leave—for me. I wasn't happy with my marriage." At this sentence I turn my head and look at her. I think, What in the world happened? Does love just end like that? How can you say you love someone, act like you love someone, and then just go away? I am so confused. I am too afraid to ask her my questions, though. She continues, "I didn't leave because of you or William; I left for me. I didn't necessarily leave because of any one thing. I just wasn't happy in my life, and I fell in love with Tom. So far, it has been the best decision I have ever made. I know it has been hard on you and William. I realize that. I feel bad about that factor."

"Don't you miss Dad at all?"

She looks at me in the dim dashboard light and says, "No"

87

She doesn't say anything more, but I keep thinking about her and Tom, and about them together as a couple. "Well, Mom, what is life like down there? What do you do? What is it like living in a camper? Don't you miss the horse and your house?" I ask.

She kind of laughs. "It was never my house. Maybe the things in it were—and still are—mine, but I don't miss it. The camper is small and tight, but Tom and I find it perfect for one another right now. We are happy. That's all that matters."

"How can love just end, Mom?" I ask. "If you left Dad because you stopped loving him, then you stopped loving me as well. You left me. You left William. He has been so upset without you. You abandoned us," I say with some conviction to my voice.

"I did not abandon you," she says quietly with some hurt in her voice. "I have loved you and will always love you and William. This divorce has nothing to do with you children."

I want to keep talking about this, but it's making me sad, which comes out in my voice. "I know, you said that before, but I can't help but feel strange about all of this. I have cried myself to sleep thinking I have done something wrong. I have dreamed of you being there in the morning when I wake up for school, and then when I open my eyes and reality hits, I am so deflated that you aren't there. It has been really hard for me to think you love me. Mom, . . . you don't even call me on the phone."

"You know I don't call you because I don't have the money for phone calls. Tom and I are starting over. We are starting from scratch. I don't have anything, Jean. That is why I am hoping you will continue to call me," she says weakly.

We fall silent for a good half hour. We are each in our own little world. About three in the morning we stop to go to the bathroom and get a cup of coffee and a little breakfast. Neither of us is very hungry, but we know we need a break. When we get back on the road, she starts to talk about her days and what she does to fill them. She is looking for a job and thinks she has found one. She is not going to go to work, though, until after I go back to Minnesota. She continues talking about things we could do together while I am visiting. She mentions a beach in Kentucky and some tourist-type stuff in the area.

I think about these ideas and activities and it makes me excited to be in her life and to be included in her plans.

Even so, with all the talk of plans and her new life, in my seventeen-year-old brain I keep missing what we once had. I miss our family. I miss our summer family vacations and when we went fishing. I am biased. I love my dad. I love my mom. I want my family back together. I don't want my dad living in Minnesota and my mom living in Brookport, Illinois. This is not right.

I am happy to be with her, though. I have even liked driving through the night, but I feel funny. I feel like I am being ripped in two pieces. I feel conflicted. I don't necessarily feel abandoned right now, at this minute, because I am with her and we are talking about things we would like to do, but my feelings of being alone are close to the surface. They are just subdued for the moment.

July – Norway

As I look to my right, I am surrounded by tall pine trees, green grasses, little white wildflowers, and jutting rocks. I hear the wind rustling the branches, and I am aware of the sounds of the bells on the big-horned sheep. There are goats here on the mountain, too, and I can hear their bleating as they move from one area to another grazing on the grass. I can also hear the gurgle of a small stream as it makes its way down the moderate slope. I see three waterfalls cascading down the mountains that rise magnificently around me. I am surrounded by God's glorious beauty. I look to the left, and I can see the lush green valley below me where my grandmother's first cousin Olav has a house.

I spot a fallen log and sit down, telling myself I need a little breather. I haven't had much alone time since we arrived in Norway, and I am grateful for some time without all the family around. My mind immediately gravitates to the few weeks prior, when I was in southern Illinois with Mom. I feel a twinge of sadness filter through me when this thought comes to mind. My desire was to have a great two-week time frame with Mom. Sadly, I didn't experience the familiar feeling of love and family that I was used to feeling. I still feel love for my mom, but there was definitely something missing—and I got homesick. After I had been in Illinois for ten days or so, I ended up crying. I couldn't explain to Mom what I was feeling. I just didn't have the words. We took a walk in the hot June sun, and we tried to talk it out, but what came out of that conversation was me just being sad. I told her I loved her. I told her I missed Dad and William. I told her I missed my dog. I ended up leaving before the two weeks were up. That nasty word "abandonment" entered my mind, but as much as I have felt abandoned, I didn't want to admit that maybe that was the cause of my homesickness. I still felt abandoned—even though I was with her. My eyes suddenly fill with tears as these thoughts swirl around, but I shake my head. Come on, Jean, I think to myself, get over it. You are in Norway. Live life in the moment, don't dwell. I look around me at the view, and I am in love with the splendor I see facing me.

Man, does Olav ever have a beautiful site for his home. When you look around, he is surrounded by four high, cascading waterfalls. Grandma told me she spent a year here when she was ten years old. She went to school with her cousins. She is full of stories, and it was fun to listen to her last night. She was talking excitedly in Norwegian, but she would take a break and tell Patricia Diane and me, in English, what she was saying. It was cool. I loved listening to her.

After breakfast this morning I just wanted to be alone for a while, so I excused myself and went for a hike in the mountains. At the moment, I have paused in my descent back down to the farm. Sitting on my log in the sun, I am just absorbing all the sights and sounds. The trip has been fabulous so far, and we really have had a great experience. The relatives I have met have been fantastic. They have been so accommodating, friendly, and kind. This afternoon, one of our cousins, Jarle, and another cousin are driving us to Evanger, which, if I understood correctly, is about a half hour away from here. We are going to visit an old church where Grandma's great-grandparents are buried. Those must be some really old gravestones.

I hear my name being called. I had better get going. I feel kind of sad to leave my view and my alone time. It has been a nice interlude in my busy vacation, but I am smiling as I quickly walk back down the hill to Olav's house.

My cousin Jarle is driving us through the mountains in his sporty little green car that Patricia Diane and I have dubbed the "Green Tornado." We have been giggling about everything today, including Jarle's car. I bet Jarle thinks we are a couple of sillies! While we are driving, Patricia Diane and I are making up lyrics to a song about being on vacation. Jarle is putting in his two cents, and the lyrics are getting pretty silly, but it's been a great way to spend the time in the car. We sure have laughed at our own juvenile lyrics.

Grandma said as we were leaving Olav's house that we would be heading up to Evanger, which is a small village in the Eksingedal area where the farm, Ekse, still stands. Ekse was where my great-grand-father, Mathias Simonson (grandma's father), was born. Grandma says the old buildings are gone, but the foundation of the old barn is still there.

We are moving quite fast along these winding mountain roads, and I am quite happy but getting kind of car sick. I wonder if we will be arriving soon. Shortly after I think these thoughts, Jarle slows down by a large white house, near a red barn and a long stone-fence kind of thing. We get out of the car, and it feels good to stretch even though the ride has not been that long. Grandma is so excited, her face is full of animation. Smiling, she hurriedly gets out of the car and walks toward the stone foundation with my aunt.

I start ambling slowly to the foundation and think to myself, These are just some old stones. As I approach, I hear Grandma explaining to my aunt, "These are the stones that made up the foundation of the old barn. This is the land where my grandfather grew up," she says in awe as we all look at the old boulders.

"Come, girls. Let's get our picture taken closer to the barn foundation," Grandma calls out excitedly.

I start to walk in Grandma's direction, and she looks at me. "Oh no, Jean, just Karen and Patricia Diane for this photo. It's a three-generation picture," she says kind of matter-of-factly.

My initial reaction to this sentence (at least for the first second) is to just ignore it, but all of a sudden realization dawns on me: I am not blood. She doesn't want me in the photo because I am not blood. For the first time in my life, I feel kind of dirty, like I don't belong. It is the strangest feeling in the world. The tears spring to my eyes and my grandpa notices.

I quickly turn my back to the whole group and move around to the other side of the van (we had brought two cars up to Evanger) in order to compose myself. Grandpa comes up beside me and hugs me to his chest. (This is not a common activity for my grandpa, who usually doesn't show too much emotion.) Because I realize this action is not common behavior, it makes me feel even more emotional.

"She doesn't realize what she said," he points out with a pained look on his face.

"That just isn't true, Grandpa. She knows what she said. She knows what she wants. I am not what she wants," I whisper sadly.

He hears my whisper of disbelief and says, "You must ignore this, Jean. You are our granddaughter just as much as Patricia Diane is. This was an unfortunate slip of the tongue."

"Grandpa, I don't know what to say. I just know I am hurt." I give him a squeeze and a watery smile before I walk away from him and go back to the car.

I pull myself together, but the rest of the afternoon, through all the pictures that are taken and the family sites we visit, I feel alone yet again. I am surrounded by relatives, but I feel alone.

As I sit staring out the car window, Patricia Diane questions me, "Jean, are you okay? What's wrong?"

"I am just tired, I think. I got a little carsick earlier when we were going up the mountain. I think I just feel like going back to Olav's and maybe even taking a nap," I answer. I turn back to the window. Gazing out, I watch the passing mountains. She must have realized I didn't feel like talking. She looks out her own window on the drive back to Olav's.

It is hard for me to do, but I force myself to bounce back—at least somewhat—after a few hours. My heart hurts, but I am strong— maybe even resilient. I stay away from Grandma the rest of the day. I do, however, cling to my grandpa's side. He is aware of my feelings and is kind hearted.

As I lie in bed thinking tonight, I realize my grandfather and I understood each other and communicated greatly through silence during the day, and my respect for him grows immensely.

Chapter 16: 1983–1985 – "Who am I?"
Jean

Fall 1983 – Goodbye, Dreams

I have just found out I am pregnant. I am sitting in my friend Sue's bathroom and have just read the stick that has turned blue. I can feel the tears forming in my eyes. I stare at the white-tiled floor wishing it would swallow me whole. The first thought I have is: *What do I do now?* The one thing I thought would never happen to me, has happened.

I received my Associate of Arts degree in the spring of 1982 and transferred all my credits to the University of Minnesota. This last year of college life at the university and sorority life have been exceptional. Being a member of a sorority and a little sister to a fraternity has given me experiences I never thought possible as I grew up. I met a guy . . . a great guy.

Going through the "rush" process to become a member of a sorority on the Minneapolis campus was not a great experience. It seems the only thing some of the houses were interested in was what my dad did for a living and how much money we had. When I met the girls at Lambda Delta Phi on the St. Paul campus, though, they seemed so much more down-to-earth, friendly, and gracious. Last fall, after I had pledged the sorority, our house was paired with the neighboring frat house down the street, Alpha Gamma Rho, for the U of M homecoming parade.

One particular night, members of both houses were together drinking beer and "pomping" the float at the beef pavilion on the St. Paul campus. Pomping was the expression we used for taking small squares of colored tissue paper and gluing them into the small octagons of chicken wire. I was working next to a cute guy, and I asked him for a tool that was near him. He handed me the tool, and I quickly responded with "manga tak." He knew what I said. Not everyone knows how to say thank you in Norwegian. He asked me if I was Norwegian, and I smiled and said "ya." That turned into a fun conversation about Norway and growing up in a Norwegian culture, and we discovered that we had both been in Norway at the exact some time, during the month of July in 1979. He introduced himself.

His name is Andrew, and he is a member of the fraternity. We didn't start dating right away, but a few months later we were a couple. We really complement one another.

This last summer we were separated because I decided to go to summer school in North Dakota. It was great to come home to St. Paul campus again and get back into the routine of university life and being with Andrew. I had missed him so much over the summer. We have been almost inseparable during this last month.

I walk slowly out of the bathroom, take one look at Sue, and burst into tears. She runs over to me and wraps her arms around me in a hug.

"It's going to be okay, Jean," she says, her voice choked with emotion.

"I just never thought this would happen to me," I cry into her shoulder. I don't say anything for a few minutes, and then I speak. "I guess I need to tell Andrew, but I am not sure how to tell him. He is even younger than I am, and I know he is not ready to take on a wife and a child."

"Maybe you should talk to your parents, first, Jean. Let them know what happened, and see what they say," Sue says.

Hmm, my parents, I think to myself. I know I can tell Mom. She will be upset, but I think she will be supportive. Then I think about my dad. He will be angry. I don't think I can face him today. I might have to tell him another day when I feel a bit stronger. Right now, I just can't even think. Right now, all I want to do is crawl into bed and sleep, and hope that this bad dream will go away. Sue and I talk a little, and I decide I should call Mom.

"Sue, do you mind if I use your phone to call Mom? I don't want to go back to the sorority house and tell Mom from there, standing in the middle of the hallway on the phone with everyone walking by. I don't want anyone to hear me tell her."

"Sure, go ahead. Use the phone; it will be okay. I will go do some homework while you tell her." She smiles encouragingly as she walks down the hall. "I will be in my bedroom if you need anything."

I dial Mom's number, and when I hear her voice at the other end say "Hello," I just break down in uncontrollable sobs. "Jean, whatever is the matter?" she asks in a panic-stricken voice.

"I have done something you aren't going to like, Mom," I cry through tears. "I wasn't feeling very well for the last two weeks, and I didn't get my period. I bought one of those home pregnancy tests, and I did the test this morning. The stick says I am pregnant," I say in a voice barely above a whisper.

There is a long silence at the other end of the line. I am still crying at my end. I feel awful. Then I hear my mom's voice say, "Jean Marie, let's just take this one day at a time. First, you need to get a hold of yourself. You need to take a deep breath and calm down."

I hear her voice, and it is calming; it isn't yelling at me. I am feeling a bit surprised that I don't hear more anger. "Are you mad, Mom?" I ask.

"We don't need to discuss how I feel right now. For today, let me help you as much as I can. I do know that I won't feel comfortable until you go see a doctor to confirm your suspicion. I can't do anything from Illinois, but maybe you can go see one of the campus doctors. I think you should also go see a counselor. I don't know how they handle these kinds of things when you are a college student, but I imagine there are campus services that will help you out. For right now, I want you to do that on Monday morning after your classes. Do you think you can do that?"

I respond in a meek voice, "Yes, Mama."

We talk a little bit more about how I am feeling—primarily about the morning sickness. I tell her a little bit more about Andrew and me and how close we have gotten during the past month. At the end of the conversation, she says to me, "Jean, I have one more thing to say. You might not want to hear this, but you should consider giving the baby up for adoption."

This last remark astounds me. "Mom, how could you say that to me? Why are you saying that?"

"Listen, your pregnancy has come at a time when you are not ready for it. You still have college to consider. You can't go to classes, be in a sorority, and have a baby. It's just not going to work. But I am not here to make that decision for you. I am not advocating for abortion. I do not believe in it since I have adopted you, and I love you. I doubt very much if Andrew will decide to marry you. You both are too young. So all I am asking you to do is consider adoption. There are so many married couples out there that cannot conceive a child," she reasons.

"Okay, Mom, I will consider it," I say unconvincingly. Then I disconnect the call.

I spend the rest of the day with Sue. She is so terrific at listening. Her composed demeanor is much appreciated. We drive around and talk. We converse about a lot of different subjects, but we keep coming back to the one topic that is fresh in our minds. She is being so wonderful and so helpful right now. I am so glad I am with her. I don't want to go back to the sorority and pretend like nothing is wrong. *How am I going to fake it?* I ask myself.

Monday nights are traditional sorority and fraternity meeting nights. *Tonight's the night I need to tell Andrew. I just can't wait any more. It's been a week since I told my mom. I owe him an explanation of my quiet and sickly behavior.* I am sitting in my bunk at the sorority, waiting for my own meeting to start in about an hour, and I don't feel well at all. I know I am going to be sick. I really don't feel like going to the meeting. As I am lying down on my bunk with my feet on my pillow, thoughts are racing through my mind.

I have thought so much about what Mom said on the phone over a week ago. I ended up calling her back on Tuesday last week to ask her to think about an idea I had. I asked her if I could come down to Illinois and go to college at Southern Illinois University for my senior year. I even suggested living with them during the pregnancy and commuting to classes. She said I could do that, but she wants me to continue to think about whether or not I am going to keep this baby or give it up. She is not telling me which way to go. She says the decision is mine, but after our first conversation, I know she would rather I give the child up for adoption.

I am struggling with thoughts of giving my baby up. I don't know how my birth mother handed me over. Every time I think about it, I get tears in my eyes. Now that I am faced with my own decision, my mind is whirling and spinning out countless scenarios. Eating is difficult, and sleeping is out of the question during the quiet of the night—sleep only comes when I am in class. Go figure that one out. My nausea is extreme. The only things I can even tolerate are cranberry juice and peanut butter toast. Anything else just comes back up. It's ridiculous. My sorority sisters are starting to ask questions. I keep telling them I am just getting over the flu.

I don't want to tell Andrew, but he has a right to know he has fathered a child. We haven't been dating that long, really only since May, but from May to August we were apart. He was in Europe the whole month of May, and then, when he came home, I left for Dickinson, North Dakota, to retake an algebra class. We called each other often and wrote letters. Some of his letters still smell like him. I love when he sprays his cologne on the paper, because it reminds me of being with him. I think I love Andrew, but I am not sure. I don't know what love really is. Am I ready to be a mother? What do I want from Andrew? I ask myself these questions, and my mind remains blank. I don't know what I want. I only know I need to at least tell him.

I still dream about going to New York and working for a fashion magazine. A year and a half ago, when I was still in Rochester, right before I graduated with my AA degree, I went on a retail merchandising trip to New York City. I loved it, in part because I got credit for going, but it was also a fantastic trip. As part of the accreditation for the class, I was required to request an informational interview from a list of contacts from various places we were going to visit while in the city. I decided to request my interview from a guy at Seventeen magazine. I remember that day so well. I was so excited to be at the magazine, and he was such a nice guy. He took me down to the room where they file the photographers' negatives, which are filed by issue. I remember being so enthusiastic and animated, and I even made him laugh a couple of times when we were chatting.

I remember that, when I got home from that trip, I wrote my guide a really nice thank-you letter and told him how thrilled I would be to work for Seventeen in the photography department once I graduated from college. He sent me a letter back telling me he enjoyed my enthusiasm and eagerness. He also told me all about an entry-level job or internship that could be mine if I decided I wanted it. I was so excited when I got that letter. Screaming was all my dad heard when I ran into the house with the mail that day. Telling him all about the interview and my thank-you letter—and then reading to him what my response letter said—did not bring the results I thought it would. Dad wasn't excited at all.

He even said, "Absolutely not! You are not going to New York. You, my dear, would get eaten alive in a city that big."

"But, Dad, this is real. I am growing up. I can do that job. It's the chance of a lifetime. Please let me go," I begged.

"No, Jean, you are not going. End of discussion, dear. Don't get yourself all wound up about going to New York." And he went back to reading the newspaper.

As I lie here in my sorority bunk, I touch my still-flat belly, and I feel just as shattered—maybe even more—as I did that day Dad told me I couldn't go. I was still holding onto that dream. I was telling myself that I would have a better opportunity with a four-year degree, and I was still entertaining those thoughts. Now, New York is definitely not in the cards for me. I feel my dreams have shattered just as sharply as a glass smashes to smithereens when thrown to the floor. Andrew's dreams, I fear, will be shattered as well when I tell him the news.

A short time later, I hunt down the president of our sorority and tell her I am pretty ill and am not going to make it to our Monday night meeting. She seems to understand and doesn't ask too many questions. I slip out the back door, trying not to be noticed, and walk over to Andrew's fraternity. It isn't quite time for his meeting to start, so I ask to speak to him.

Andrew comes outside and sees me. "My meeting is about to start, Jean, can we talk later?" he asks.

"No, I have something I need to talk to you about," I say somberly as my eyes fill with tears.

He comes over to me and gives me a hug. He looks into my eyes and says softly, "What is it?"

"I don't want to ruin your life, Andrew; I don't want to be that girlfriend who destroys any chance you have at happiness." I pause because I am so afraid. My knees are shaking, and I feel like I am going to lose everything inside of myself. "I am pregnant," I state in a voice barely above a whisper.

He doesn't say anything. He just pulls me tighter to his chest in a hug. I am afraid to look into his eyes to read them, as my head is buried in his shoulder.

Then he responds, "Look, everything is going to be okay. We will get through this. It might be tough, but we can do it."

We chat a little bit about how I am feeling and about my visit to the doctor who confirmed my pregnancy. It is still early in the pregnancy, and I outline the options of abortion, adoption, and keeping the baby. Then I say, "Mom has offered up a solution. She and I have discussed the option of me leaving the university and coming to Illinois to finish up my degree, at least while I am pregnant. We have discussed adoption."

"Wait, wait, wait," Andrew says with intensity. "When did you find out you were pregnant?"

I take a deep a breath and say, "A little over a week ago."

"Why are you finally telling me now?"

"I don't want to ruin your life, Andrew. You are younger than I am, and you have a lot longer to go with college than I do. I was trying to spare you."

He looks at me fiercely and says, "You are carrying my child, too, Jean. You should have come to me right away. I don't want you to move to Illinois. I don't want you to take my child away from me. I don't want you to give my child to someone else to raise. This situation we find ourselves in is just as much my responsibility as it is yours."

I break down in full tears. I have really been trying not to cry hard, but at this last exchange, I can't help it any more. Andrew spends some time calming me down, and we talk some more. We say good night to each other, and, as I leave the front yard of the fraternity, I am feeling a little better than I have all day.

It's so cold out here, I think as I stand outside of the smoke-filled kitchen on the back doorstep. Andrew and I are at a house party tonight. It's the weekend, and there are always lots of parties. This party is at the house of one of Andrew's friends from home. I don't know these guys very well, yet, so it's not like one of our normal frat parties, where I know everyone. There is a lot of smoking and drinking going on inside, and I needed a breath of fresh air. I am feeling so nauseated, I feel like retching right here and now. I take a deep breath of the cold air and fight the desire.

As I stand out on the back step, I run my mind over the past couple of weeks. Andrew asked me to marry him a week after I told him about the pregnancy. We have already discussed a quick wedding, and I told my dad. I told him over the phone on Saturday, and he shouted at me. I think it's the only time I have ever really heard him shout that fiercely at me. Of course I cried, but then I told him that Andrew was willing to marry me. Then, the next day—Sunday—he came up to the university. We went out for a burger at Poppin' Fresh, and I think the conversation went better because we were in a public place. By the time he dropped me off at my sorority, we had talked things out, and I called Mom to give her the update. Dad has called the church and the American Legion in Hayfield, and the wedding date is set. We are planning a December wedding during our Christmas break from school. Andrew and I also have had a chance to tell his parents. We told them together, and I received a warmer welcome than I had expected. Andrew's parents both gave me a hug and welcomed me to the family. They seem like such nice people.

I really get quite irritated sometimes when I think about this baby I am bringing into the world. It's not about the baby itself, though, just the circumstances of it all. Feeling the morning sickness all the time is getting old. I don't think anyone likes to feel like they have the flu all the time. Then I think about college. . . . It's done for me—and I won't have the degree that I want. Andrew and I have discussed it:

marriage in December, and then I go find a job in January—no more classes for me. I get teary as I think about the fact that I won't graduate. We both agree that it will be best if Andrew continues with his classes and works at the same time. I will need to find a job as soon as classes let out in December. I am a little nervous about everything and how fast it all is happening. I am getting married. I am going to have a baby. It is scary how fast one emotional decision in life can alter one's life path forever. Goodbye, New York City.

The back door opens, and it is Andrew coming outside to check on me. "Hey, what are you doing out here? It's kinda cold, Jeanne."

I smile at him when he uses my nickname. "Oh, the smoke was making me feel ill. I needed a breath of fresh air."

He wraps his arms around me and kisses me. "I missed you. I had to come looking for you. Why don't you come back inside?"

"I just wish everyone wasn't smoking. Gosh. . . . It smells so bad in there. I am sick to my stomach," I say as another wave of nausea hits me.

We stand outside the back door for a few minutes in silence, wrapped in each other's arms and grabbing a few kisses.

"My mom called me today," he says, pulling slightly away from me so he can look at my face. "Since we are getting married so fast, she wants to know if you would like to join us, the Voxland family, for Thanksgiving this year."

"Sure, Andrew, of course I would. Your parents were pretty nice to me when we told them we were going to be married—and that we are going to have a baby. I was so surprised they took the news as well as they did. They even gave me hugs. Do you want to come to my grandmother's on Sunday after Thanksgiving? That's when my dad's family is celebrating. I haven't heard anything from my mom. I don't think she is coming up to Minnesota this year," I say.

"I haven't met your grandma, yet," he says thoughtfully.

"No, not yet. I guess you will on Thanksgiving weekend if you decide to come." I smile back.

"What is she like? Do you think she will like me well enough?" he asks with a silly grin. My heart warms at his grin. I love seeing that man's dimples!

"Grandma will like you fine, Andrew. You are Norwegian and you are a Lutheran. That will be the most important thing," I say, teasing.

A thought occurs to me right then: Andrew and I have never talked about my being adopted. He doesn't know. My heart beats a little quicker, and then I realize it's not that big of a deal. There are lots of people who are adopted. He probably won't care. So I look at him and tell him that I am adopted.

He suddenly pushes me away and walks down the steps. He has a plastic cup of beer in his hand, takes a long swig, glares at me, and says, "When were you going to tell me this, Jean?"

"I just did, Andrew. I thought you should know, but it's not that big of a deal. I just thought you should know I was adopted before we got married."

"I can't believe you didn't tell me. What other secrets do you have lurking in your past? Other guys? Other babies? What more do you want to spring on me?"

"Oh, for goodness' sake, Andrew, I am adopted, not a murderer. Good grief. Why are you getting all crazy about this?"

"Because it's a secret that I didn't know about you!" he shouts.

"Well, Andrew, we haven't been together that long. I mean, we have been together since May, but in that time, you went to Europe, I went to college in Dickinson for the summer, and then when we get back to school . . . . Well, it's been kind of crazy. We have both been really busy with our fraternity and sorority stuff. The topic just never came up until I thought of it tonight," I explain. I smile at him and walk to him. He turns away from me.

"I don't know anything about you. You don't know anything about you. You don't know why you are the way you are," he declares.

"Oh, that comment and this conversation are just ludicrous, Andrew!" I say. "Really, are you going to carry on about this? Are you going to recant your offer of marriage?" I say with mock scorn in my voice.

"Of course not," he is quick to respond. "However, I am pissed off that I didn't know about it—and that I don't know about your background and heritage."

"Do you really know your full heritage, Andrew?"

"Yes, I do," he simply states.

He pushes me aside and walks back into the house out of the cold, leaving me outside. I feel the cold now. I feel the emptiness of the air since he has gone inside. I want to go home. The party has lost its allure. I don't want to be there anymore. I feel alone . . . again—which is not an unusual feeling in my little world. I know in my heart he will come around. He may not talk about it again, but for now, I am feeling alone and even slightly abandoned.

As I think about being lonesome, I get tears in my eyes. I have felt lonely quite a few times in my life, but these thoughts are darker, and I push them away. No use in dwelling on them. The bright side is that I am going to have a baby. A baby to call my own. A baby to love—and one I will never abandon. If I don't abandon this baby, my hope is that he or she will never leave me. I touch my stomach just to reassure myself.

What if Andrew changes his mind? What if Andrew thinks that my being adopted is a bigger issue than I do? All these "what if's" clog my mind. I don't want Andrew to bow out of getting married now. I gave him the opportunity to leave our relationship when I told him I was pregnant, but now . . . over my adoption? Would he ditch us, the baby and me?

The back door swings open again. Andrew sees me standing in the yard and comes toward me. He slowly walks over to me and wraps his arms around me. He gives me a hug. He does not say he is sorry, but he does say, "It's all going to be fine, Jeanne. It's all going to be fine." (I love it when he calls me Jeanne, and hearing it makes me feel a bit calmer.) His voice is muffled in my hair, and I relax into his arms, enjoying his warmth. It is all going to be beautiful. I have to have faith in the unknown and feel okay about everything.

December 23, 1983 – Our Wedding

I am getting married today. I look at myself in the mirror, then I glance at the raging snowstorm outside my bedroom window. *What a great day to get married*, I say sarcastically to myself. *This weather is crap!* I am alone right now in my bedroom. Dad is downstairs drinking coffee; William is still asleep in his bedroom. I think Dad is fine, but last night he seemed kind of anxious.

I walk into the kitchen. "Hi, Dad. . . . How are you this morning?"

He looks up from the farm magazine he is reading, "Fine, fine," he repeats. "The weather isn't all that great today, but we are going to get you married," he says with a grin.

After Dad's initial outburst of anger at my getting pregnant, he has been pretty cool. He has been supportive and helpful, and for that I am truly grateful. He has done a lot of the work for the wedding himself. He arranged for the reception to be at the American Legion, and he organized the band and the food. I think he even took care of the flowers. I am not sure who really did that task. I was at school, and between him and my aunt (his sister) it was all taken care of. I only had to find my wedding dress and bridesmaids' dresses.

I sit down at the table with him with a piece of toast in my hand, which I stare at—wondering if I have any appetite or desire to eat it. "When do you think Mom will get here?" I ask.

He looks at me sympathetically and says, "She isn't coming, Jean."

I stare at him. He must be mistaken. I couldn't have heard what I just did. There is no way a mother would miss her only daughter's wedding. "What? Not coming to her daughter's wedding? Are you kidding me?"

"She called and said she turned around. The weather made the roads slick, and the wind picked up making visibility hard on the freeway. The weather was too bad for her to travel north. She feels bad, but she isn't coming," he explains.

I automatically grab the phone and dial her number. She answers quickly, almost like she has been expecting me to call.

I don't even greet her. "How could you do this to me today, Mom? How could you leave me like this? It's my wedding day. What mother leaves her daughter on her wedding day?" I shriek at her.

She calmly answers, "The weather was just too bad, Jean. You don't want me driving up to Minnesota in a blizzard do you?"

I am dumbfounded. What God would allow a daughter to not have her mother at her wedding? Is there a God? I finally get up enough courage to continue, "I am speechless, Mom. I am completely and utterly speechless. I do not have words to explain how I feel." I can feel the tears sting my eyes. "I am going to go. I will call you soon. I will let you know how the day turns out. . . . Bye." Tears are burning in my eyes.

I hang up the phone without even waiting to hear what she has to say. Dad visibly winces when he sees my eyes. He knows. He knows, without even asking, what I am feeling: betrayed; abandoned. It's my wedding day. There is a blizzard. It's already ten below zero outside. Is anyone even going to come to this wedding? Yeah, right, I think.

I turn and look at my dad. "Okay, Dad. It's you and me. I am angry, but I will get over it. I am determined to have a great wedding, even if it is just you and me."

Dad looks at me and gives me a wink and a weak smile. "It will be a great day."

As with any wedding day, there are many happy moments. My heart is full, there is a beam of love on my face, and tears of joy form in my eyes when I see how many people braved the blizzard to be at the wedding for us. Our wedding does not have a shortage of happiness regardless of the fact that my mother isn't there—and the weather is dreadful. I reflect on the day as I wave goodbye at the door of the American Legion, and I see I am surrounded by my family, my best friends, my sorority sisters, and our fraternity brothers. All of these people made the trip through the blizzard to come to our wedding. *Perseverance!* I am honored and feel grateful for everyone in my life.

I wave excitedly to the crowd as Andrew and I embark into the cold world. I get into the already-warm cab of the truck, which Andrew had thoughtfully started. I am struck by the symbolism of our wedding day and our life together. I think to myself, All storms must end. Life goes on.

I am grateful when we get to the edge of Rochester. It usually takes about a half hour to drive to Rochester from Hayfield. With the minus-forty-degree temperatures, snow, and wind of the blizzard, it has been quite a challenging and grueling drive bucking snowdrifts and strong winds. The half-hour drive has turned into over an hour. It's my wedding night, and there's a raging blizzard outside the cab of the truck. Andrew and I are the only people on the road. I have to admit that I am scared, and my mind is prayerful as we continue on. We see a hotel up ahead, and he turns and looks at me. "Should we stop there?" he asks. Of course I don't want to—it is not the romantic night of my dreams—but I am not irresponsible, and we stop. After all, it makes the most sense.

We are supposed to stay at the Kahler Hotel in downtown Rochester tonight, but we realize we will not make it that far. This hotel on the south edge of town will have to suffice. I am happy and sad at the same time. I am happy that Andrew and I are embarking on a new adventure; I am happy and grateful that I was surrounded by brave people who put Andrew and me above their thoughts of the weather. But I am feeling sad about the way it turned out—no Mom. I am also worried about my wedding guests, and I hope for their safe arrival at their own homes and Christmas destinations.

I wake up the next morning to bright sunshine and a very white world. It is Christmas Eve. Andrew and I will be with his family today. I am happy that, hopefully, the roads will have been plowed enough to get to his home. Andrew left the truck running all night long so that it wouldn't freeze. Thank goodness for diesel engines, right?

I look down into the parking lot from our second-floor hotel room. Andrew was not the only one who kept his vehicle running. The parking lot is full of impromptu "weather guests," and several of the cars are already warming up. We get dressed, and I give my dad a quick phone call just to let him know we are doing fine. I decide not to call my mom. I just don't want to deal with the conversation. At the same time, I am teary as I think about her not being there last night and about spending another Christmas without her. It's been four years since we spent Christmas together. It seems so long ago.

June 30, 1984 – A New Birth

Our child was born today. I am euphoric. I am exhausted, but most wonderfully elated. I am able to hold my baby in my arms, and I am filled with awe. I study every inch of her tiny body. I stare at her dark hair and am filled with wonder about her. I am filled with questions about who she looks like and what her personality is going to be like. The first hours I feel she looks just like her father. I am feeling bad about this thought for some reason. She looks like Andrew. She doesn't look like me, and I think that, secretly, I was hoping to have a tiny being that looks like her mother running around the world. But she looks like her father. Maybe she will have some of my traits as she grows? I gaze at her tiny fingers and am amazed that I created such a wonderful little being. I am in love. Who would have thought that I could fall in love so quickly?

All sorts of thoughts are running through my head. I try to rest, but it is quiet in my hospital room, and I hear the squish of rubber-soled nursing shoes on the highly polished hospital floor. I am staring at the tall, many-square-paned windows. My thoughts go to another time, twenty-two and a half years ago, to be exact. I think about a woman I don't know. What does she look like? Does she have a big smile? Does she have blue eyes like mine? Did she get married to the man who is my father? What is he like? I don't even know the color of their hair. Maybe I don't look like them, either. Maybe I won't ever look like anyone. I do have friends who don't look like their parents. I wonder if my biological mother is tall like me. My mom is a smaller woman, and I always feel so big next to her. Does my birth mother "love" like I do? I know I love easily. I get hurt easily, too. I suppose when you love easily it can backfire on you and hurt can happen just as quickly. Did she cry when she had to put her baby in the arms of a nurse who took her away? I can't imagine taking my infant and putting her into someone else's arms and never seeing her again. I start to softly weep.

I call my mom, who doesn't answer the phone because she is on her way up to Minnesota to stay with me for two weeks when the hospital discharges me. I remember this as I hang the phone up on its cradle. Still, I wonder about a woman I probably will never meet. I wonder about a man who had to give up a child of his own blood, and I wonder if he cared for the woman who gave birth to his child. I muffle my tears with a pillow and then walk over to the little infant-sized hospital bassinet. I reach in and pick up the precious life Andrew and I have created.

Andrew and I had decided that if the baby was a girl we would name her after his grandmother Terra. Her middle name is going to be Marie, just like my mom and then me. Her names will have a special meaning. I like that. Through my teary eyes, I gaze at our child, and I hug her to my chest. I look at her and say out loud, "You are mine. You are mine, and you are loved."

August 29, 1985 – An Opened File

The building I am looking at through the rain on the windshield is ominous. I know that once I walk through the doors, though my life will be the same, it will also be different. I will gain knowledge and understanding, I think. Lutheran Social Services is the agency through which I was adopted. Today, my daughter, Terra Marie, and I will enter through its doors and, maybe, I learn something about myself that I have never known.

Glancing at my watch, I see I am a bit early. But I am traveling with a one-year-old these days, and I always need to pad my time because you never know what might happen with a little one. We walk into the reception area, and the receptionist introduces herself and says, "Why don't you follow me? I will take you to the room that your social worker, Claire, has reserved for you this morning. She will be right with you."

She takes Terra and me to a toy-filled nursery. The room is crowded with small tables and chairs just perfect for small children. There are big picture windows on the south side of the room allowing the room to be bathed in light with a backdrop of rain. My daughter has never seen so many toys in one place in all of her young life. She gravitates toward them, leaving me alone with my thoughts tumbling around my head. I am fearful for some reason—fearful of the unknown, I guess. The funny thing is, I have dreamed of seeing my birth parents, but I have not dreamed of ever meeting them. You know, in the kind of daydream where you are awake but still you don't have control over where your mind goes. I have never spoken to them in my daydreams, but I have watched them from afar.

Nervousness overcomes me. I only want to open up the birth records for my daughter's sake. I don't want to interrupt anyone's life or anything like that. I have heard the horror stories of adopted children who seek their birth parents, only to find that the parents have moved on with their lives and totally reject and resent the child who is seeking them. Well, I would never open myself up to that kind of pain. I have been through enough of my own pain that I plan to steer clear from that. But, then again, I am curious enough to open a file to see what has been written about them and their family health. I have brought a child of my own into the world, and I want to find out if there is anything written in their file that we should know.

I look out the window scattered with raindrops falling down the glass on the outside, and I can see my reflection in the window. I see my face, a young face; I notice the pink-and-white striped dress, the white jacket, and the little ruffled white socks in my white shoes. I feel cold—cold either because of the rain and the dark dreary day, or because I am frightened of the past and the future all in one, and frightened of what this all represents for me.

The door opens and Claire walks in with a smile on her face, with one hand outstretched, and the other holding a file. She seems, at first glance, to be kind-hearted. I think I like her already, and she hasn't even said a word. She sits across from me at one of the children's tables in a child-size chair and even seems quite comfortable doing so. I find it endearing. Terra is oblivious to her, because she has found a little doll, as well as a baby bottle and a crib for the baby. Maybe I need to buy my daughter some accessories for her own little doll. She is adorable as she moves from one toy to the next. She looks like an angel in her sweet blue dress, white tights, and the new shoes Grandma bought her.

Claire and I make small talk for a few minutes. We talk about my daughter and what she is like as a fourteen-month-old. I admit that she moves so fast for a new little walker that I can hardly keep up with her. But today she is not running from me; she is immersed in the new toys.

Claire hands me a piece of paper filled with transcribed notes from the adoption file. I don't read the first paragraph at first. No, the first line I read states that my birth mother was fifteen years old at my birth. This possibility had never crossed my mind before. I had always pictured two people in college—like Andrew and I were when we got pregnant. This doesn't necessarily bother me, though. It is just a fact that surprises me. She was so young.

I put myself in my birth mother's shoes immediately, and I can't even fathom what she must have gone through, emotionally. I am hoping that her parents were supportive. I can only hope that she felt she was doing the right thing. At the age of fifteen, I was immersed in art, drawing, painting, photography, dogs, and horses. This thought strikes me as funny for some reason, and I laugh. Claire gives me a curious glance. I smile back at her, letting her know that, no, I was not laughing at the seriousness of what I was doing by opening up the file. Instead I feel nervous. It's nervous laughter with the sudden realization that there are outcomes and consequences to all the choices we make—a realization whose meaning stays with me for some time.

I turn my attention back to the typed page. My birth mother had a sister, which means I have an aunt I have never met. My birth father had siblings as well. I consider this fact for a bit. I am lucky in that I have relationships with my aunts and uncles. Maybe some of my relationships are a bit stronger with some aunts and uncles than with others, but I am well aware that relationships take both parties to make them work. Wow, there are more aunts and uncles out there in the world that I have never met. The typed white paper I am holding in my hands basically describes how old my birth parents and their siblings were and what work my birth parents were doing, and also gives a small amount of information about their health, including stating that my birth mother was allergic to wool. Now I know why I hated that Christmas outfit Mom made me wear. I itched so much every time I wore it, and Mom didn't understand. I get it now. It says my birth mom had a good sense of humor, and that my birth father liked sports. I find the typed words fascinating.

There is silence as I read. The only sounds we hear are Terra playing with the dolls. I feel like crying and am not sure why I don't.

"What are your thoughts, Jean?" Claire asks.

"I am feeling sorry for myself, I think. My thoughts are all jumbled. I feel fear, but don't know why. I don't fear you, though. I just have this creepy fear thing in my chest," I say thoughtfully.

"Adoption emotions are real, Jean. Everyone is different. Everyone takes hearing the truth a little differently. Is there anything in what you read that is surprising?"

"Umm . . . that is a hard question to answer because I feel emotional, but I think it's the heritage information that is confusing. My mom always told me I was Norwegian, which is only partially true. I was brought up in a very Norwegian family with Norwegian traditions. I always just took it for granted that I was Norwegian and nothing else. I think my grandmother will be disappointed in that." I say this to the floor. I can't meet Claire's eyes because my words sound stupid. But I really feel that way. I don't want Grandma to find out I opened this file and found out the truth about myself. I feel that she will not ever want to talk to me or be with me if she knows this about me.

"Jean, you do have some Norwegian heritage from your birth parents. But you also have German and Bohemian blood in you. Many Americans, and even Europeans, do have heritage mixtures within them," Claire counters matter-of-factly.

"True, you are right, but I have never given it much thought. Now, someday Terra—and possibly other children I may have—will ask what their nationality is. Andrew is mostly Scandinavian. There is nothing wrong with what I am; it's just new. I am going to have to go to the library and look up what 'Bohemian' is. I am not sure I know." I stumble over my words. They don't come out very smoothly. Then I think of my uncle Milford, and I smile because I know he is Bohemian and proud of his heritage.

"Is there anything else about what you have read that you would like to discuss?" Claire asks.

I reply, "Is this all there is? Is this all the file has in it?"

"Yes, that is all there is. You are one of the lucky ones in that someone took the time to put that much information into the file. There are many adoptees who come to open their files, and the only thing they find is a birth certificate," she says. "What were you hoping for?"

"I'm not sure. I am happy I came and opened the file, but I am also feeling sad and kind of blue. Maybe I was hoping for . . . more. Maybe I wanted to feel like I would know a little about them and therefore a little more about me. Or, maybe I just feel blue because of the weather?" I pause, then say, "I am not sure how to process this."

Claire smiles at me and says, "Every situation is unique. What you're feeling is normal, like I said before. Where do you want to go with this information? Do you want to write a letter for the file? I also understand the pain of rejection. None of us want to feel that. It is a risk our heart takes when we choose an unknown path." Claire pauses, then says, "Do you want to leave contact information in case one of your birth parents wants to find you? Or do you want us to arrange a meeting with them?"

Suddenly I feel panicked. "No meeting!" I quickly state. I look at her thoughtfully, then say, "I would be willing to put contact information in the file, though. I am not one who will go seeking, but I know that if they wanted to contact me through you—call me on the phone sometime, send me a letter—I would be receptive."

"Would you be willing to meet in person?" she asks.

"Not right now, but then again, maybe I would someday," I say.

She gets up from the table and crosses over to a desk. She pulls out a note pad and a pen and gives them to me. Terra comes over to me then, and I allow her to grab the pen away from me. She puts her own little drawing on the note pad, and I add my name to it with a brief note about contact information. It is the best I can do in the moment.

"Are you satisfied today, Jean? Do you feel like you did the right thing? I am only asking because you seem quiet and reserved. I am worried about your reaction to all of this," Claire says.

"Oh, yes. Of course I am happy I opened the file. I am surprised by some of the information, but then . . . life is full of surprises, isn't it?" I say with a weak smile. I am ready to go home. I feel tired, and I now want to just go home and kind of process my new, tiny bit of information.

The rain has stopped when I buckle my daughter into her car seat. It seems the sun is trying to peek around the clouds. When we arrive back at our apartment, I go through the motions of changing our clothes, making some lunch, playing a little bit with my daughter, and then rocking her to sleep in the rocker. I put her into her crib with a light kiss on her forehead. As I walk back to the living room, I can feel the emotion start deep down in my chest, and in a few minutes, in the silence of the afternoon, I finally let the tears fall. The emotional tears of finding out and knowing just a tiny bit about myself has hit me. I fall into an exhausted emotional sleep on the couch with the typed white paper in my hands.

Chapter 17: 2002 – Pheasant Hunting
Dennis

Man, is it cold out here. I am walking in a cornfield somewhere in the middle of South Dakota hunting for pheasants. I don't hear much of anything at the moment. Everyone in the hunting party is all pretty quiet, keeping on the lookout for pheasants. The dogs are a bit antsy. They know what is going on and are feeling the anticipation. They are alert to any noise in the field. Despite the cold and wind, I am content to be with my son, brothers, and nephews. There is even a sense of relief after going through the past year.

Fifteen minutes go by, and my thoughts go from memories of the past year to memories of many years ago—and a lost love. I'm brought back to the present when I hear a rustle of grass not too far ahead of me. I cock the hammer of my shotgun in preparation for a bird possibly flying up in front of me. My muscles are tensed, my ears are trained on the faint sounds, and my eyes are focused in the direction I thought I heard movement. I shift my weight, and—without warning—one of the dogs lunges forward in my peripheral vision. I turn my attention to that commotion, and a shot rings out from my brother's direction. A flock of birds surges up in flight, and shots are heard, including from my own gun. Suddenly the dogs are set free, barking, and chaos ensues. Four birds are brought back by the dogs within a short period of time.

As a group, we decide to head back to the lodge for dinner and maybe a game of poker or two. I clean up, don some clean, warm clothes and go downstairs to meet my son, brothers, and nephews in front of the lodge's big fieldstone fireplace. My older brother is the only one in front of the fireplace when I walk into the room.

I grin and greet him, "Feel better? Warmed up after the hot shower?"

"The shower felt great," he says as he grins back at me. "The late afternoon cold was settling in on me, and I'm feeling much better. How about you, Dennis?"

"I definitely am warmed up. I'm also ready for some hot food, cards, and maybe an Arnie Palmer," I respond with a grin.

"I can smell the food. It's making me hungry. Ready to lose in poker tonight, brother?"

"Who's ready to lose? Not me. I'm feeling lucky tonight."

"At least you are feeling luck in cards," he says. "How are you doing—really? I mean as far as all the other issues in your life go?"

"It's been a rough year, and the best thing about it was my three kids, Stacia, Chandler, and Kyle. I am grateful for them. They are the best," I say, looking right into his eyes. When he catches my eye, he understands how the year has been. But I am ready for the future—no matter what it brings—as long as the kids are good and seem okay through this whole ordeal. Failure is not falling down, it is staying down.

Turning to the fire and staring into the flames, I say rather quietly, "Do you know what I did two weeks ago?"

My brother laughs and says, "I can't imagine what you did, Dennis. What was it?"

I look him in the eye and say, "I drove to Brownton."

"Okay," he says rather slowly, thinking about his choice of words. "I am not sure I should ask, but . . . why?"

"I got it in my head that I wanted to see where Karen lived when we were kids. I drove around the town, kind of reliving memories, thinking about the kids with whom we went to high school, remembering the basketball games, track meets, football games, dances, and the sodas at the hotel. It made me think I was going nuts, but maybe I just wanted to remember something happy. The only problem is I felt some happiness with those memories, but it also brought up some stuff that maybe I don't want to remember. I do think about Karen now and then. I think about what might have been had we gotten together." I say, and my serious tone surprises both of us a little.

My brother looks at me thoughtfully. "Dennis, it's been a rough year for you. You are not crazy. Just as you said: you were looking for the bright side. It makes sense. When you were with Karen, you were happy. I get it." He pauses for a moment, then asks, "What did you like about her, Dennis? What attracted you to her—and why do you still think about her?"

Now that is a question, but an easy question for me to answer. "She was just everything I liked and wanted in a person: smart, loving, warm, sincere, and really kind-hearted."

I walk over to the side table at the far end of the room and pour myself a glass of tea with some lemonade in it. I take a long swig, and my brother meets me at the table and pours himself a glass of tea. He drinks it pretty swiftly, and there is a pause in our conversation. He lifts his glass and says with a smile, "Cheers, bro. Cheers for a better year." I lift my glass to his and softly clink the glass.

Just then, my son and nephew come down the steps laughing. They greet us, and one of them asks, "Hey, what's the cheers for?" The evening begins and turns from serious conversation to some all-around fun with joking around and playing poker.

Years before, on another hunting trip, my dad, my brother Vance, my brother's friend, and I will go to Lac Qui Parle in Minnesota to go goose hunting. One night, as we are sitting around the campfire drinking and smoking cigars, the three of us will stare into the fire and start to talk small talk.

My brother will say to me, "Do you ever wonder and look up Karen to see what she is up to?"

With sadness in my voice, I will tell him, "No, I don't know anything about her."

My dad will bring up both Karen and Denise as he is staring into the fire and ask, "Whatever happened to the baby?"

I will answer, "She was adopted by a very nice family. That's all I know."

There have been many hunting and fishing trips where conversations will sometimes turn serious in the course of a weekend. I am grateful for my family, and through all of the trials and tribulations I have been through in my life, my younger brother, Vance, and I had many discussions. During those hunting and fishing trips from northern Minnesota to Wyoming, Canada, and Lake Michigan, it was easy to have conversations that ranged from good natured teasing to the serious. He helped me get through the difficult times with his understanding nature and compassion for his older brother.

Chapter 18: 2013 – Mom Is Gone
Jean

The sights and sounds of the Minnesota State Fair are so familiar to me that sometimes going there feels like I am coming home. I have spent so much time during the last thirty years attending the fair with Andrew and his family. It's been fun. Besides doing all the entertaining things one does at the fair, I have spent most of my time in the swine barn, touring the 4-H building, wandering through the art building, and getting my annual helping of gyros, my favorite fair food.

I am standing by the show ring, watching the 4-H kids bring in the pigs they have raised. I am looking forward to seeing how my niece and nephew do with their pigs this year. I'm misty eyed as I sit and think about years ago when my own girls showed their pigs. I am enjoying seeing my niece and nephew show, but I'm remembering my own girls and all the showing they did over the years. For some reason, I am missing those days.

I hear my cell phone ring over the noise in the swine barn. The caller readout says it is Mom's husband, Tom. Why is Tom calling? I wonder. As I prepare to say hello, my heart automatically quickens.

"Hello," I say quickly.

"Hey, Jean, it's Tom. Am I bothering you?" he says.

"I am at the State Fair, but I can talk. Is everything okay?" I ask. It is unusual for him to call me—Mom usually does—so I feel that there is something wrong.

"Well, no, everything is not okay." He pauses, and then says, "Your mom fell this morning. She got a pretty big bump on her head, and I took her to the emergency room. She is going to have to stay here at the hospital for a few days."

I hear those few words, and I have a hard time comprehending what he is saying. For some reason my brain isn't working very quickly. "Tom, how did she fall? What happened?" I ask. I can't believe the conversation is happening. It's almost like my mind is working too slowly. I feel dim-witted, like a movie that is running in slow motion.

"She fell at the house this morning when I was out on one of my service calls. I was close by the house, thank goodness. She called me, and I ran her to the emergency room right away. Jean, your mom broke her neck," he says kind of slowly. At least I think he says it slowly. Maybe it is just taking my mind that long to process what he says. "She is resting quietly at the moment, and she knows I am talking to you. She told me to tell you she is fine. They have put her in a neck stabilizer so she can't move her head. She is also in some pain, and they have given her medication for that."

"I should come down there right away!" I exclaim with tears welling up in my eyes.

"No, if you are at the fair, just enjoy the fair. You can come down to see her tomorrow. She is stable right now and resting. The doctors are going to keep her on some medication to keep her resting for today, to keep her neck still, and then wean her off that medication tomorrow."

"Are you sure?" I ask. "I feel like I should come right away." I feel like I'm about to become hysterical.

"Jean, she is fine. Just come tomorrow. That will be soon enough," he responds calmly.

We talk about specifics just a little more and then hang up. I stand by the cement wall at the south end of the barn and stare out into the hot August heat, listening to the heavy traffic noises on Como Avenue. Andrew is inside watching the pig show, and I feel like I just want to melt against him. I am suddenly so very tired and unsure of how to feel.

I am certainly grateful that my mom is fine, but a broken neck is something that I don't know anything about. I am feeling emotional because I don't have any information about recovery statistics. I am so uncertain that, when I think of her having a broken neck, it triggers unwanted feelings and thoughts. I am worried and relieved at the same time. It feels so weird.

I'm not sure how long I have been standing there when I hear my youngest daughter, Hanna, come up to me and say, "Mom, McKenna is going to show her pig. She is in the holding pen. Come inside and get some pictures."

"Oh, let me grab my camera and get some shots of her," I say. The emotions of the phone call must not be showing on my face, or else Hanna just is too preoccupied to notice. Either way, I'm happy I don't have to say anything right at that moment.

I go back inside the barn and try to enjoy taking pictures of my niece and nephew showing their pigs. The time between each pig arriving in the ring gives me time to kind of process what Tom has said. All sorts of thoughts are swirling around my head: What will Mom look like when I go see her? Is she going to be alright? Can she talk and comprehend? I don't have any answers. . . . I feel like I want to leave right away.

Once the pig show is over, Andrew and I grab some lunch with Hanna, while our middle daughter, Laura, heads for home. Laura is pregnant so I don't blame her for wanting to get home and off her feet.

After a state fair lunch of gyros, Andrew and I start for home. I am hot and looking forward to getting back out to the slightly cooler air of the country. Once in the car, I finally tell Andrew what has been bothering me: that Mom has fallen and broken her neck. We chat about it, but it is just general conversation. While we wait in traffic to exit the parking lot, I say, "Andrew, I am scared."

He knows what I am referring to. He knows me so well. "Don't make any judgments until you see her, Jean. It won't do you any good to get yourself worked up right now," he says rather understatedly.

"I am going down to the hospital tomorrow, Andrew," I say. I say it with conviction in my voice because I don't want anyone to try to stop me from seeing my mom.

"I will come with you, Jean," he says in a flat, almost unemotional tone.

I am surprised. I hadn't necessarily been expecting him to come to the hospital with me. "Are you sure?" I ask. "You usually don't want to come with me when I do hospital visits and those kinds of things."

"She is your mom, Jean. Yes, I will come with you."

I wonder if I have hurt his feelings, but I don't say anything. Silence permeates the air in the car on the way home. Each of us is lost in our own thoughts. Minnesota Public Radio plays softly in the background during our ride home. I am grateful for the sound, allowing me to acknowledge, to no one in particular, that I don't feel like talking.

The very next day, on a bright, warm August morning, Andrew and I arrive at the hospital in Ames, Iowa. As he locks the doors of the car, I am struck with nervousness, jitters, and nausea. I walk at a steady pace, but my steps do not feel light; they feel heavy. I am so nervous.

Tom gave me some directions, telling me where to go once I got to the hospital. Having followed my notes telling me which elevator to take and which floor she is on, I notice Tom coming to meet us as we exit the elevator. He greets us with a smile, and I give him a hard hug. He seems okay so far. I was imagining something different.

"Hi, Jean. Hi, Andrew. Before you go in, just let me tell you a little bit, maybe give you a heads up as to what you will see. She has a large dark-purple bruise in the middle of her forehead from when she fell. She tripped and fell forward when she was getting out of her chair. When her head hit the floor, the impact caused her neck to break. Besides the bruise, she is in a neck brace to hold her head in place so she heals correctly. She is in pain, but she is also on medication for it. She knows you are coming, and she is looking forward to seeing you." He pauses, and then looks at me.

I am speechless. I do not have words. I can't even come up with any. Instead, I simply look him in the eye and nod my head. I had thought in the car about the times Mama had been in the hospital during my childhood, and I can only think of one time—when I was in fourth grade, and she fell on the ice and broke her hip. Over the last five to ten years or so, she has fallen and hurt herself, mainly her back or ribs. She is tiny and rather delicate. But, over the course of healing for each fall, she has persevered and come through each one okay. I remember being scared when I was a child, scared when she had hurt her back . . . but that was nothing compared to what I am feeling today as I follow Tom into Mom's hospital room.

Sappy me, I immediately start to cry when I see her frail, slight body in her big hospital bed surrounded by a big neck brace, and I see her black eyes and bruised forehead. She looks like she has gotten into a barroom brawl. She smiles at me, though, right before her own eyes fill with tears. I know she has never wanted me to see her in this kind of state.

"Hey, Mama," I say with a grin through my own watery eyes. "Gosh, . . . Mom." I whisper in her ear as I lean in to give her a kiss. I can't hug her. She is in too much pain for me to touch her, but I do kiss her cheek and reach out to hold her hand.

"It's so good to see you, Jean and Andrew. Thank you both for coming to see me." Her voice is not strong, barely above a whisper. She is shaky as she speaks. She looks at me with watery eyes and says, "I hate it when you see me like this. I am fine, though. I know I look like a train wreck but . . . really . . . I am fine."

"Gosh, Mom—you don't have to be so brave. But I am glad the nurses and Tom are keeping you comfortable. Mama . . . ," then my eyes fill with tears and I start to cry. I can't help it. I can't hold them in any longer.

"Jean, don't cry. Everything is fine. Everything is going to be okay." She tells me this like the trooper that she always has been and always will be. "I will get better; it might take a while, but I will be fine. I am not worried," she says in her slight, soft, whispery voice.

"Mama, the girls are worried about you, and they all send you love and hugs. I called them, and I also called William. He is worried about you, too," I manage to compose myself enough to say. William lives in Dallas, Texas, and I know he is worried about Mom. He wants to come up and see her in the hospital but his work is keeping him from coming to Iowa.

She smiles at that and says, "You tell them thank you for the kind words and spiritual hugs. Call William back and tell him not to worry." She takes a moment before asking, "How is the weather in Minnesota? Has it been hot?"

That last comment of hers makes me smile, and I make up my mind that I won't dwell on the obvious. Apparently she wants to talk about other things, so we make small talk about the State Fair, the hot weather, and how the pigs are handling it all. Andrew and I stay at her bedside with Tom for a little over an hour, and then Andrew and I decide she is getting exhausted entertaining us. We feel like she needs to get some rest, so we say our goodbyes.

As I stand at the doorway of the room, I say, "Mom, I am coming back tomorrow. I am not sure if Andrew will, but I am." I think she smiles at me, but she is dozing off as we turn to leave. Tom walks us to the elevator.

"So what are you thinking, Jean?" he asks.

"I am coming back tomorrow, Tom. I have an immense need to be with her, see her, and talk to her." The drive from our home in Kenyon to Ames is about a three-and-a-half-hour drive. I know Andrew and I will drive the three hours home this afternoon, and I will turn around and drive the three hours again tomorrow morning, but this thought does not bother me. I just know I want to be with my mom.

"Okay," he says. "I thought you might say that, so this is the plan. I have a local customer I am going to help since you are coming down. We can tag team tomorrow. The plan from the doctor is to move your mom to a recovery floor of the hospital instead of ICU. They feel she is stable enough for the move to recovery. If you are coming down, I will stay with her until you arrive, and then you can be with her on your own for a while. I will come back after I go check on this customer."

"That sounds good, Tom. I will leave right away in the morning. I will get down to Iowa as soon as I can."

"See you then. If anything changes, I will give you a call," he says and turns to go back to Mom's room.

The drive home is quiet. Andrew and I are both lost in our own thoughts. I have gone from feeling sad and scared to feeling tired and numb. I guess there is a part of me that also feels relieved that this hurdle has been crossed, and that I can go see Mom again tomorrow.

It is Monday, September ninth. It has been two weeks since Mom fell, and she is home from the hospital. I took the day off work to be with her today. She has made some great improvements over the last couple of weeks, and today Tom has decided to go on some calls that are farther from home. I came down to be with Mom for the day so he could go to some of those calls.

We have had a great day so far. She is in a little better mood than the last time I saw her, and we have talked about everything under the sun, including a few stories about her childhood and her father. He died young, and I love hearing stories about the grandfather I never knew. She makes him come alive for me. I made her one of her favorite salads for lunch today, but she didn't have much of an appetite. I guess it's the medication that makes her not want to eat anything. I think she ate only three or four bites of the salad.

I look at her in her chair, and her eyes are closed. She needs a bit of rest, so I do the lunch dishes and change the linens on the bed while she naps. When I pass her, I gaze at her tiny form, her head encased in a neck brace, resting in her chair. She seems so small. She weighed only eighty-five pounds at her last weigh-in at the hospital. She has been losing weight because she has no appetite due to the medication they are giving her. She says that nothing tastes good to her. For goodness' sake, she couldn't afford to lose weight before she fell, I think to myself.

Gosh, she gave me such a scare two weeks ago. I feel like I have aged. I definitely feel the tables have turned in our relationship. I am now the caregiver. This is not a position I am used to being in. I am accustomed to being the daughter who calls her mother and shares recipes or anecdotes about the kids, maybe looking for answers to a few questions, and then also whining about some tiny little thing while Mom responds with smiles through the phone and gives me answers to my questions or words of encouragement.

While I am running the Swiffer over the tiled floor, I hear Mom stir. I walk over to her and smile.

"Hi, Mom, did you have a good rest?"

"Yes, thanks. I did. I am sorry I fell asleep on you."

"For goodness' sake, Mother," I say. "You are recuperating. You need your rest—and you don't need to entertain me. What else can I do for you? Is there anything you need? Are you hungry? Do you want a bite of anything?" I ask hopefully.

She looks at me and gives me a child-like look. "No. I am not hungry."

"Maybe I can entice you with some ice cream or strawberries?" I ask. Mom loves ice cream and strawberries. She always has.

She turns up her nose and says, "Not today. Not in the mood for them."

We chat about other small, insignificant things, like what I had done to keep myself busy while she slept. I tell her about washing dishes, changing bed linens, running a load of laundry, and Swiffering the floor. Then she looks at me and says, "You know I love you, don't you?"

"Of course, I know you love me." I laugh.

"Well, I just want you to know you are a godsend, and I am appreciative of the time you are taking, and have taken these last two weeks, to be with me and help me out," she says.

"Of course, Mom, why wouldn't I? I am your daughter, and I care about you and love you!" I say with a smile of conviction.

"Oh, I know," she responds. "But I do know some people who have daughters that wouldn't come so far, take time off from work, and do the things you have done for me. I am just glad you are here. You make me feel much better when you are around."

I have no idea where my next words come from, but I say without thought to them—or their repercussions: "Mom, do you have any regrets? Regrets about adopting William and me; regrets about marrying Dad; regrets about the divorce and leaving to be with Tom?"

"Well, you asked me that question before, Jean, a long time ago. And, if you remember, I told you then—and am going to tell you now—I do not have any regrets. I am happy in my life. I am happy with the choices I made. I may have small regrets about a few things but certainly not about marrying Tom. We have built a great life together. I also do not have regrets about adopting you and William. You are my children, and I love both of you very much. Both of you have been bright spots of joy in my life," she says. "I know how much you hurt when I left your dad, but I had to leave for myself. I couldn't be a good mother to you if I was unhappy in my life. I felt it would be better for both of you if I left and tried a different route to happiness. I have tried to be there for you in your times of trouble. I feel you have made some hard but good decisions about your own life. I am proud of you. You are capable, Jean, of dealing with all the complications life has to offer. Life throws us all kinds of curve balls. We just have to get through them. Like me falling; . . . I need to heal and then move on."

"I have felt your love, Mom, but I also have felt deserted at some points too. It's rather hard sometimes to think about those times because I don't want to feel deserted," I say kind of quietly.

"I can understand that, even though it hurts me to hear you say it. Just know you are always loved—and that I feel you are a wonderful person. It was never my intention for you to feel deserted or alone," she says with a smile.

"Not every memory is bad, is it, Mom? I mean, with you and Dad. Did you enjoy our family vacations and holidays? I don't want to think, when I look at the pictures, that you were unhappy."

She kind of smiles, and maybe just to appease me, she says, "No, not every memory is bad. I have good memories of our camping trips, fishing trips, holiday traditions, birthday parties, and summer picnics. Maybe, Jean, all of the trials we have been through as a family were just meant to make you stronger. I don't have to worry about you. You have a good head on your shoulders. You are a good wife and mother. Your memories are happy ones, so keep them close to you. Continue to be positive. We all make mistakes, but I guess what we need to do is just remember them and try to learn from them."

I liked her last sentence, and it made me smile at her. "Today has been a good day, Mama," I say. "We haven't really talked so openly lately."

"I have enjoyed our conversation as well. We haven't really been alone for a whole day in a long time," she says. Then she changes the topic of conversation to supper and what she thinks I should make for Tom.

The rest of the afternoon is spent just doing odd jobs for Mom and chatting. The topics range from the grandchildren to her great-grand-children and everything in-between. She asks all kinds of little questions about them and states her love for them as well.

I stay overnight with her so I can be around to help out in the morning. I help Mom with getting dressed and other small chores. It's Tuesday, and I need to drive the three hours home to Kenyon in Minnesota from their home in Jewell, Iowa, so that I can work tomorrow. When Tom comes home for lunch, I leave.

As I drive the long stretch of freeway, I reflect on the conversations Mom and I have had, and I feel calm. I feel a sense of love and peace. It was so wonderful to chat with Mom about everything that we did. Even though I know I will see her again in a week—or maybe as soon as the weekend—I am still a little worried about her recovery. But today I feel good. Yesterday was a wonderful day full of conversation and words of love.

William called, but I missed him; I hate missing his calls. I decide to stop for coffee and call my brother to update him on Mom's recovery. We have a good conversation, and he says maybe in a few weeks he can get away from his job to come to see Mom.

Two weeks ago, Mom and I spent our incredible day together. We talked about so many things, and even discussed our plans for her complete recovery. Today, however, I am gazing at my small, frail, motionless mama lying in her bed in a hospice. My eyes are dry at the moment, but the last few days my mom has truly deteriorated. Little did I know that the wonderful Monday we spent together would be the last real conversation I would ever have with my mom. As I think about it, my eyes get watery yet again. I am still hopeful that maybe she will turn a corner in her healing and open her eyes. I am sitting beside her bed, holding her hand. When I notice any little movement from her fingers or deeper breathing, my heart quickens and I get excited. Nothing has happened though. Nothing has changed in a very long time, and she has not opened her eyes.

It is quiet in her hospice room. People don't talk much in hospice. It's rather eerie, and I am sometimes uncomfortable. The room is dim. There is a window, but the curtains are drawn. There is a small lamp glowing near Mom's head. Tom is sitting next to her on the other side of the bed holding her other hand. We are sitting here together in silence. I suppose we are both hoping, but we are not discussing, not talking. Time is slowly passing, and I am wondering if she will open her eyes if I go to the bathroom. Or, if I leave her, will she squeeze Tom's hand and not mine? Will I fail to catch something big? Will I miss something I don't want to miss? I am scared to leave my chair. I am even scared to leave the room to go call Andrew, who is waiting for a phone call from me to let him know how I am—and how Mom is doing.

Tom says something to me, but what he says doesn't register with me.

"What? Sorry, I missed that, Tom."

"I said," he looks at me and states quietly, "that we need to prepare ourselves for the worst. There is a possibility she won't make it through the night, Jean."

"Why do you say that, Tom?" I ask incredulously. It seems impossible to hear this from him—through all of this, he has been my source of hope.

"The nurse said something to me last night, trying to prepare me," he utters in a low voice.

He says some other things in a quiet voice, but my mind is not registering what he says. I go into myself and can feel the walls starting to crumble. The walls of self-defense that I have held together the last few days are starting to crack. I excuse myself from him and run through the hallway to the door that leads into what I call a "peace garden." A grief counselor spoke with me yesterday when we were moving Mom here, and she told me that if I needed peace and quiet, I should go out there. The minute my feet hit the stone pathway, I can feel my stomach lurch, my chest heave, and the wall break. I fall to the ground amidst the fall leaves and flowers.

Thoughts, pictures, memories, songs . . . everything going through my mind is so chaotic. My brain is fuzzy. I can't concentrate because all I see is her face—her face when I was young. I feel her hands touch me when I had a fever, and when she hugged me or smoothed the hair from my face. I hear her voice comforting me over a boy who had broken up with me and then I hear her gentle response when I told her I was going to have a baby. I hear her laughter when I ejected and spewed a full mouthful of apple cider vinegar all over the kitchen walls. Then I remember her unshed tears when she left me in Rochester to start a new adventure of her own. It is the sight of her unshed tears which causes my own breakdown. My own reserve crumbles, and the tears come, wild with fury and anger.

"Mama, . . . you just can't abandon me again! You just can't. . . . I didn't have enough of you. I need you. I want you to come back to me." I weep as I beat the stone pathway with my fist and collapse, face down, in the grass of the peace garden, amidst the flowers, in a fit of crazed moans and heart-wrenching sobs.

I drive home after my scene in the peace garden. My eyes stay dry as I am driving, but when I see Andrew, I run into his arms and break down. We don't say anything as he strokes my back and just lets me cry.

At four the next morning, my mama passes away. As I realize the truth of this, I also realize that I didn't even get to really say goodbye because I wasn't going to give up my hope, even though, maybe deep down, I knew it was the end.

Chapter 19: 2014 – Divorce
Dennis

Karen and I lost contact with each other for many years, except for one time when I took her to lunch at a Chi-Chi's Mexican restaurant on Grand Avenue in St. Paul. The reason for the lunch was that, on June 4, 1984, I had gone into treatment for alcoholism. In the AA program, there are twelve steps, which, if followed, will change your life. The eighth step is to make a list of all of the people you have harmed and to make amends to all of those people. So I felt that I needed to make amends to Karen. I guessed that she seldom thought of me because she was with another guy, but I thought of her—and I had to make amends and apologize.

The next time I saw Karen was at International Market Square in Minneapolis, when her husband was having his own troubles with alcohol. She obviously knew I was in the AA program, and so we met to have a cup of coffee. It was really great to see her.

In all the years that followed that last meeting—not knowing anything about Karen—when my wife and I would travel around the country or the world (to Disneyland; Branson, Missouri; or New York), when I saw a mother holding onto a child's hand or heard the name "Denise," I would wonder if it was my daughter.

I always kept a soft spot in my heart for Karen, even though I was married for thirty-some years to another woman. I went to therapy for seven years with a psychologist to talk about Karen and Denise, among other issues. I guess I was a fool for thinking that Karen still had feelings for me, especially since she didn't know whether I was alive or dead. And I don't think she cared.

Even though my first marriage ended in divorce, I was blessed with three wonderful children whom I love and respect very much.

They are all successful in their endeavors. I also have two wonderful daughters-in-law and six wonderful grandchildren from that marriage.

After the divorce, however, I was devastated—because, to me, divorce had never been an option—and it was a life-altering event. My mind would go to Brownton, Karen, and Denise. I would get in the car and drive the forty-nine miles from home in Eden Prairie (a Minneapolis suburb) to Brownton. I would drive through town and travel with my memories. It felt good to be back home and remember the love with which I had been blessed.

I was politically involved in Eden Prairie and campaigning for the reelection of Senator Norm Coleman. Even though I lived in Eden Prairie, I took some brochures to the neighborhood in St. Paul where I thought Karen might live, but I did not find her. After that night, I drove to Brownton one last time, knowing even as I did that she wasn't there. I just had to drive around her house. After that, I gave up on her, thinking it was kind of silly of me. I remember feeling empty and sad. I had tried so hard to locate her, but nothing prevailed.

The next time I saw Karen was at the Brownton All-School Reunion at the Lake Marion Ballroom, in 1993. We danced, but I could not accompany her home because she was married and was there with her mother. I did ask whether I could take her home and just talk, but she said she couldn't because her mother was there. I was, again, rejected by her.

Over the past twenty years, I really lost touch with Karen.

The party I went to last weekend really opened up a door of possibilities for me. I am glad we played the game, and that I was curious enough to look Karen up on LinkedIn—and then even to take the step to call her on the phone. I have been divorced for fifteen years, and I am excited about reconnecting with my lost love.

We have been communicating by phone and e-mail for three months. The feelings I have are definitely love—but we needed to work out the logistics. Karen and I both have mentioned in our phone conversations that we are both set in our ways.

So we are now using the word "compromise."

Chapter 20: 2014 – Third Time's a Charm
Karen

In 1997, I took a job in Washington State and moved there with my husband and son. Seventeen years later—on Monday, October 27, 2014—I was at work when I got a message that an old friend named "Denny" had called for me, leaving a number beginning with a "612" area code. The only Denny I knew who might have had a 612 area code was my first love, so I called him back immediately saying, "How did you find me?"

It was so good to hear his voice; it has not changed at all. But what does he look like after all these years?

I am now a widow and he is divorced, so we decided to continue to communicate and exchange contact information. I go home from work after we talk and google him. His hair is silver in the picture I find of him, but he still has the great smile that I always loved and the same twinkle in his eyes.

Is our relationship going to rekindle after all these years? We are seventeen hundred miles apart. How will that work? I suggest we e-mail, talk, and text to get to know each other again. Our phone conversations sometimes last for an hour or more, so the physical distance between us doesn't seem too great as we get to know each other again.

One night, during one of our long conversations, the subject turns to marriage in general. Knowing that he has been divorced for fifteen years—and that he has had relationships with several women, including a five-year live-in situation—I ask the question: "Would you ever get married again?"

He replies, "No, I like living alone now with my little dog. I know where everything is in my townhome."

So I say, "Then I guess you wouldn't ask me to marry you again, would you?"

His answer is: "It's like baseball; three strikes and you're out."

I counter with: "I have a different take on it: the third time's a charm!"

He hesitates briefly and says, "Well, if you put it that way!"

After that night we have several conversations regarding marriage. We still have not seen each other for almost twenty years, and we are still seventeen hundred miles apart. Are we compatible enough to get married? Dennis suggests that he could come to visit me in January of 2015 when he takes what he calls the "West Coast Swing," visiting his daughter and grandson in California and his son and daughter-in-law and two grandchildren in Oregon. He says he could continue up the west coast to see me, and we could then decide whether marriage is an option.

The Pacific Northwest typically doesn't have very cold weather. However, one day when I am particularly chilled, I pull out a box of my "Minnesota winter clothes" and choose a beautiful yellow sweater to wear to work. It is the warmest item I have, plus it has a beautiful memory associated with it because it was a Christmas gift from my first love many years earlier.

"What a pretty sweater you're wearing today, Karen. Where did you get it?" one of my co-workers asks.

"You aren't going to believe it, but this sweater was a Christmas gift from my boyfriend—in 1959," I answer.

"You've got to be kidding!" she says, surprised.

"Who keep clothes around that long?" asks another co-worker as she joins in the conversation.

I want to tell my co-workers all about the phone call from Dennis a couple of months earlier, but our conversation is interrupted by the phone ringing. Later, after thinking about the whole electronic courtship Dennis and I are having, I decide to keep quiet about it until we determine where our relationship is going to end up.

The holiday season is upon us now, and Dennis and I especially miss being together during this time of year. I remember Dennis saying this is the last Christmas we will be apart, and he has suggested we get married in Las Vegas in April when he will be traveling there for a trade show. I could fly down to join him, and we could get married in one of the chapels there.

I google "How to get married in Las Vegas" and report my findings to him.

His response is, "Why wait until April? Let's get married in January when I come to visit."

So he has now downloaded a Washington State marriage license application, had it notarized, and sent it to me to take to the courthouse. There is a three-day waiting period, and the license is good for sixty days. We figure if things don't seem right for us when we get together, we can always postpone it.

For now, our plans to marry in January are moving forward, and we plan to have Dennis's two sons come to Washington to be our witnesses.

Chapter 21: 2015 – We Finally Meet
Dennis

Every year I take what I call the "West Coast Swing." I fly from Minneapolis to Los Angeles to visit my daughter and grandson. From there, I fly to Portland to visit my son, daughter-in-law, and two grandkids.

This special year, 2015, after Portland, I am flying to Seattle on January twentieth.

When I first told my daughter, Stacia, I was getting married, she asked, "Why don't you wait for a couple of months to see whether or not you get along with each other?" My two boys said "Whatever makes you happy, Dad. We will support you and back you up 100%."

Karen is going to meet me at the airport in Seattle. In our conversation last night, she asked, "Dennis, how am I going to recognize you?"

I chuckled and said, "Well, I don't have brown hair any longer; I have silver hair. Think that will be enough for you to figure it out?"

She just laughed.

When I arrive at the airport in Seattle, the scene is something you might see in a movie. Think about it in slow motion. Karen pulls up to the curb in the passenger pick-up area. She gets out of the car, runs to my arms, and—for the first time in almost fifty years—we kiss. My love has been found. We go to her house, and we talk for hours. We get married two days later.

After we get married, we stay in Washington State for a couple of weeks just getting reacquainted. I have to fly home to Minnesota for a business meeting, but we talk to each other on the phone several times a day and decide that being apart is hard on both of us. After some discussion, Karen agrees to move to Eden Prairie with me.

One Sunday, we take an afternoon drive to Brownton. Driving that road for the first time after getting married, we feel wonderful. When we got to the two-block-long downtown, we park the car by the City Meat Market and try to find the initials that we carved in the brick fifty-four years earlier. We drive around Karen's old house, the school, and some old friends' homes. The biggest difference between when we were teenagers and now is the fact that we now speak of our feelings and the love we have for each other.

We talk about Denise as we drive around town, and I bring up the topic of doing a search for our daughter. I guess one of the main reasons we want to look for our daughter is to find out if she was alive, but also to find out if she is well, if she is married with a family, what she does for a livelihood, and—if she is married—what her husband does. In the past, I had asked Karen a couple of times to find our daughter, Denise. Now it is *our* time to find her.

We contact Lutheran Social Services, go to the office for an interview, and that day they prepare us for the future. They begin by preparing us for the worst, saying that Denise may not want to see us—she may not want to have a relationship after all these years. They are also positive, however, letting us know that at our daughter's age, fifty-four, she may be more open to seeing us because her adoptive parents may have passed away or may be in a nursing home.

Although this is an emotional process, we were aware that Lutheran Social Services charges a fee of almost one thousand dollars for parent/child searches. Karen and I wrote them a letter explaining our situation, though, and the search committee feels it is so lovely—and that our story is so touching—that they waive the entire fee.

Within weeks, we receive a call from a case worker. She explains that they located our daughter within forty-five days. At first, our daughter's husband, a man named Andrew, was reluctant to even mention to Denise that her birth parents were searching for her. He thought it was a scam, because every time he tried to call the number that had been left with the message, it went into voicemail. Luckily, he eventually called the number of Lutheran Social Services to verify the name of the case worker, and found it was legitimate.

Chapter 22: 2015 – Reunited, Again
Karen

I picked Dennis up at the airport in Seattle on January 20, 2015. I recognized him instantly by his beautiful silver hair and his stylish attire—he has always had excellent taste in clothing. As tired as we were that night, we had a long talk and decided to go through with getting married. I had originally scheduled the civil ceremony to be the following Saturday—and Dennis's sons planned to fly in to be our witnesses. Last-minute changes with his sons' work plans prevented their coming to Seattle, however, and the judge also had a conflict. The judge was available Thursday, January 22, at 11:00 in the morning, though, and asked whether that would work. We could make it then, but we had no witnesses.

My first thought was to ask my closest neighbors, Dick and Helen, to be our witnesses, but I didn't want to ask them over the phone. They had no idea about Dennis—or my communications with him—so I told them I had a friend from Minnesota in town who wanted to meet them and set a time for them to come to visit Wednesday afternoon. However, the next afternoon, I got a call from my neighbors saying they had car trouble and couldn't meet.

"Well, how about coffee at nine o'clock Thursday morning?" I ask. They respond, "We can make coffee."

Our wedding ceremony is scheduled for 11:00 Thursday, so we can make that work. I introduce Dennis to my neighbors the next morning, and we briefly chat.

I eventually ask them, "What are you doing at eleven o'clock this morning? We are getting married. Will you be our witnesses?"

"Oh my gosh, you two! Are you really going to get married?" they ask excitedly.

My neighbors are excited and hurriedly get ready to leave for the courthouse when Helen asks, "What are you doing for flowers?"

"It's just a civil ceremony; I don't need flowers," I answer.

She says, "Yes, you do. Let's stop to get a bouquet.."

So we stop to buy a grocery store variety bouquet, and Helen breaks off the long stems and wraps a pink ribbon around the flowers as we drive. We get to the courthouse and are greeted by a man in jeans, tennis shoes, and a sweatshirt asking us for our paperwork. Within minutes, the same gentleman comes back with a robe over his jeans—he is apparently also the judge—and commences with the five-minute ceremony.

After we are married, my husband asks the big question: "Now can we go on a date?"

Everyone laughs at the fact that after all these years we have been together only three days before getting married—and that we are now going on our first date together in forty-nine years.

The receptionist who originally took Dennis's call is so moved by our story of getting together after all these years that she asks if she can write a human interest story for the local newspaper, *The Everett Herald*, about us. We agree, and she e-mails it to the newsroom several days later.

Within minutes of her sending the e-mail, she receives a call from one of the paper's columnists. "Where can I interview this couple?" the columnist asks. "I want to run it in the Sunday paper the day after Valentine's Day."

Since Dennis has gone back to Minnesota now, and I am still in Washington, the columnist interviews him by phone, but I visit her in her office for an interview. She asks a lot of questions.

"Do you have any old photos of the two of you together in high school?" she asks.

"No, I don't think either of us saved any photos of us together."

Later, as Dennis and I speak on the phone, he suggests looking in our high school yearbooks for photos. In the back of one of my yearbooks I find a love note from Dennis. No photos of us together are found, but our individual class photos are used in the newspaper along with article, titled "It Took Decades to Find and Marry His Very First Love."

During one of our many phone conversations leading up to our marriage, Dennis had asked me if I ever thought about Denise and about looking for her. I answered "Yes, I think about her, but I don't think it is fair to her to enter into her life at this point after all these years." He continues to press the issue, saying it would be nice to know if she is alive and where she lives. He says that maybe she needs us for medical reasons. Maybe she is curious about us and has tried and failed to find us. I knew he wanted to find her, and—I have to admit—I was curious, too. However, with our traveling between Minnesota and Washington to get the Washington property ready to sell, we were not in a position to start the search to find her.

The house in Washington, where I had lived with my late husband and our son for eighteen years, needed a lot of work before we could put it on the market. Dennis and I trimmed bushes and had trees removed as well as having the pasture mowed to keep the blackberries at bay. Although the realtor had a long list of improvements that were suggested in order to bring the property to the level it should be before listing it for sale, we decided to sell it "as-is" rather than spend the time and money to make the repairs. We were anxious to move my belongings to Minnesota, but Dennis's townhome was too small to squeeze in any of my furniture. We chose to store select pieces in a self-storage unit until we could decide where we were going to live. I brought some clothes and personal items and moved to Eden Prairie, Minnesota, with the intention of moving the rest of my belongings when we found a different place to live.

Once we are somewhat settled in Dennis's townhome, he again brings up the subject of finding our daughter.

"Now that I found you, there is one piece missing," he says. "If we could find our daughter, our family would be complete."

I finally give in, and we proceed by filling out an application at Lutheran Social Services in St. Paul to begin the search. We meet with

Susan, who describes the process and advises us to keep an open mind about the whole situation. She explains that they may not find our daughter, that she may no longer be alive, or that she may not even wish to see or hear from us. After hearing the pros and cons, we are prepared for the worst. We are asked to write a letter to the post-adoption staff telling our story—and why we want to find our daughter. We are also asked for a check to pay the fee to begin the process.

We write our letter from our hearts and explain to the committee why we gave our daughter up for adoption at the ages of fifteen and seventeen—and explain that we are now together again fifty-four years later. The staff, emotionally moved by our story, returns our check, saying they will provide their services free of charge.

We are also asked to write a letter that can be sent to our daughter if they find her—and to include a photo of us—which we gladly provided. The letter we write starts with "Dear Daughter" and goes on to describe what we were like as teenagers and why we chose to give her up for adoption rather than to have an abortion, as well as offering our personal descriptions, hobbies, interests, and some information about our current lives and how we have reunited after so many years.

One day, while we are shopping at a mall, I get a call from the case worker in charge of finding Denise. The voice on the phone says, "Karen, I think we found her."

My heart skips a beat, and I say, "Where is she?"

"I can't tell you that, yet, but do I have your permission to reach out to her?"

"Of course, you can," I respond, eager to tell Dennis the news.

He, too, is excited to know more about the daughter we had together nearly fifty-five years earlier. We are told by the case worker that Denise's name was changed by her adoptive parents to Jean, and that she will place a phone call to Jean on our behalf. She cautions us to not get too excited, yet, as Jean may or may not want to meet us or hear from us.

A number of days—that seem like an eternity—go by while we wait for news of our daughter. We find ourselves thinking the worst, but hoping for the best. Then the call comes that Jean is reluctant to meet us but will write us a letter—and possibly meet us with the case worker present at Lutheran Social Services, which is perfectly okay with us. In the meantime, the "Dear Daughter" letter is sent to her, along with the photos.

A five-page, hand-written letter from Denise/Jean, arrives in the mail on a day when Dennis is out of town on a business trip. A college roommate is visiting with me when the letter arrives, and, seeing my excitement, she urges me to open it. It doesn't take long, reading about Jean's thoughts, family, etc., before my eyes well up with tears of happiness.

Jean has included a photo of herself and also one of her husband, Andrew. Looking at her photo, I can see her eyes and her facial features are identical to Dennis's. I pick up a photo of Dennis in his army uniform from the bookshelf and hand the two photos to my friend. Her comment is, "There's no doubt that she is his daughter!" The resemblance is amazing.

In her letter, Jean suggests several dates that she and her husband are available to meet with us at Lutheran Social Services. When Dennis comes home and reads the letter, he immediately says, "Make the appointment for the first day they are available."

Chapter 23: 2016 – The Letter
Andrew

I pull up to the mailbox and let the ubiquitous gravel dust clear the car before I open the window to get the daily mail. It's a dry April afternoon, and the local farmers' implements have turned the hard gravel into a fine powder. I open the metal mailbox and push my arm in to pull out a neatly folded pack of mail. It contains the usual stuff and propaganda, bills, the Kenyon *Leader*, and a few letters.

I drive down the driveway and start to sort out the wheat from the chaff, deciding what mail to throw out in the garage and what to take into the house. There is a strange hand-written letter to my wife. It's interesting because it has no return address other than a P.O. Box, and there are five digits written on the lower left of the envelope. I also notice the ZIP code, 55108, which is one that we lived in when we were in college. That number has been encoded into my brain for years, as my wife, Jean, and I went to college at the University of Minnesota. She was a member of the Lambda Delta Phi sorority, and I was a member of the Alpha Gamma Rho fraternity, just a couple of doors away from each other with the same ZIP code.

I usually don't open my wife's mail, but this one piques my curiosity to no end. Hand-written address, a St. Paul ZIP code, numbers written at the bottom left-hand side of the envelope—it all leads me to question the contents. This, to me, looks like trouble, and I am not about to allow this to affect my wife in any adverse way. It dawns on me that the ZIP code is also the site of Lutheran Social Services.

I know that Jean was placed up for adoption when she was born, and Lutheran Social Services was the organization that facilitated that transaction. We have no idea who, what, or where she came from, or her lineage—and coming from a farm background, history is important to me. I was raised on a farm and we were taught that history and genetics go hand in hand. Genetics are a peek into the past and predictors of the future. We don't know what kind of history her birth family possessed. Are there health concerns that might be passed on to our children? I know all of my past, but Jean's real history is shrouded. Of course, Lutheran Social Services was also just down the street from the first tiny apartment we occupied when we were first married, so my thoughts about the letter could be completely off target.

With all the oddities on the envelope, I could have very easily decide to toss it in the recycle bin before I take it into the house. Curiosity gets the best of me, however, so I decide to open the letter. When I open the letter and read that "someone in your family would like to get in contact with you . . . ," my first thought is that it sounds like the biggest scam of the century.

Finding this a bit perplexing—since I believe I know all of her relatives—I call my brother, who is a detective for our county, and ask if he's heard of any recent scams to folks in the community. He tells me that he hasn't, but that it is still possible that this could be a scam. I have had recent conversations with fellow co-workers of people who have been scammed recently, so I am still a bit concerned. Even so, in the far reaches of my mind there is the faint thought that this could be real. Perhaps . . . perhaps someone from her past—a father or mother—could be looking for their long-lost daughter. I proceed to open the letter, knowing both scenarios could be possible.

Jean comes home, and we have our normal discussions about how the day went at work and talk about what to have for supper. After a bit of small talk, I fess up to opening a letter sent to her.

I laugh and say, "It was more than likely that crazy cousin of yours, and they finally came with a straight jacket."

Jean reads the letter and says, "I'm too tired to think about anything like this; you can do with it whatever you want," and she tosses the letter back at me.

I don't push the subject any more that evening.

I take the letter to work with me and file it in my desk drawer. I figure it will be best to call from a phone that couldn't or wouldn't be traced back to our home—just in case this is some kind of quack looking for money. I read and re-read the letter, hoping I will find some hidden meaning or clue to what it could be. My mind spins and churns around at a dizzying pace about all the possibilities of what it could mean, considering all kinds of odd scenarios from one end of the spectrum to the other. Still, in the back of my mind, I'm thinking this could actually be someone looking to find or re-connect with Jean. If it is, then they'll have to get past me, first. I ask myself, Can I flush out this person who has this supposed "information on a family member" without telling Jean? Will I open up a Pandora's box whose contents I can't put back? What if it's the real deal?

The next day I call the number on the letter, and after two rings it goes to voice mail. That's a red flag for me, but at least the person's greeting on her voice mail matches the name on the letter. Her voice message says she'll be "in the office from 8:00 till 5:00; please leave a message." Well, there's no way that I'm going to leave a message for a complete stranger who sends out letters with such an equivocal and mysterious tone. I don't leave a message, and I put the letter back in my desk. Still, the idea of what this could be about lingers—not just in my mind, but in my gut where the feeling burns away, even though I don't have anything but faith and hope to go by. Maybe I'll try again tomorrow.

After not sleeping all that much, I am back at work and thinking over things and decide to call again. I place the call around nine in the morning, and again my call rings twice and goes to voice mail. I try again after lunch, and still my call goes to voice mail. Alright, I'll call just before leaving from work. Again, two rings and I'm sent to voice mail.

I have now been calling for almost two weeks, three calls a day, and I'm getting frustrated. Maybe the letter writer is out sick, on maternity leave, or on vacation—or perhaps it truly is some scam. The scam idea starts to permeate my thoughts as I grow a little disillusioned of the possibility that this could be what I suspected all along. I will have to open myself up to the potential of disappointment if this is just a phony scam or something else.

At home, I tell Jean that I've been attempting to contact our mysterious letter writer, to no avail. I ask, "Jean, should I pursue this any further, or just let it go?"

"Go ahead and try calling the number again next week, Andrew, but you and I have both discussed that this could be a scam. A parent to come looking for me after all this time," she pauses, "I doubt it."

I let it go and drop the subject, as far as Jean knows. But when I start something, I'm going to see it through till the end, no matter what the outcome might be. My curiosity level has been piqued—at this point it's off the charts—and I hate not knowing the facts. Why does this veiled woman want to get a hold of Jean? She said it was important, but this will have to wait till Monday, and I'll try again.

Monday rolls around, and I open up my desk drawer and pull out the letter. I must have read it twenty times by now and still can't get some of my anxieties out of my head, so I decide to call again. Will my results be the same as they have been in the past? My hope fades as I place the call. Again, two rings and voice mail. I'm putting the letter away, perhaps for the last time, as I listen to the voice mail, and at the end of the message I start to put the phone down. I guess I could say that I did the best I could, and then that would be history. But something from the back recesses of my mind tells me to leave a message. I'm still not convinced, so I hatch a plan: I decide that I'll leave a message—but give her a wrong phone number. That'll add a bit of intrigue to the dog-chasing-his-own-tail mystery with which I've been dealing. Two can play at this game.

"Hello, I am Jean's husband. We are concerned about this 'important message' that you have waiting for her. Call me at this number," I say into the recorder, giving her a wrong number to call me back. If they really, really want to contact Jean, they could call the house phone. "We're in the phone book," I tell her as I complete my message, and I hang up.

I am impatient and think to myself, *I'll let her stew on this for a while and let her do a little detective work if it is so darn important.* The ball is in her court.

A couple of days have gone by, and I haven't called the number listed on the letter. The notion that this would proceed to a next stage has been put out of my mind. It's done and over with—what we don't know won't hurt us.

I get home Wednesday afternoon, pour myself a beverage, and sit down in my old leather chair, sunken to one side by years of repeated routine. I turn on my iPad to look up the weather forecast and notice that the house phone has a number of missed calls—and a new message. I quickly look through the missed calls and dismiss all of them as I don't recognize any of the area codes. I press "delete all," and they're gone. I then press the voice mail message and let it play as I go to the refrigerator for some more ice. I faintly hear the message, and think I hear a lady say that she called the number I left the other day, but that the number had been disconnected. Is this the mystery woman? I press the key to re-play the message and listen again. To my surprise, it is. She says that she did, in fact, call the number I left. I guess she took the bait—finally looking for Jean in the phone book. The ball is in my hands now. Do I pursue calling her number, or have her call us back? I figure I'll call her again and see if I can connect, but that will be another day.

I tell Jean that evening: "That mystery woman called the house phone today. Let's listen to the message." We listen to her voice message together. We read the letter again and discuss all manner of possibilities of who, what, and why.

After our discussion, Jean says with apprehension, "Andrew, you can call her back. You handle this matter so I don't have to deal with it."

I call the number for Nichole, our mystery woman, again on Thursday and leave another message, this time leaving my real office number. I wonder if she'll call me and not the home number. The message is for Jean, but—being protective of my wife—I want to handle this alone. Around ten in the morning, Nichole calls. I know all of Jean's cousins, aunts, and uncles, so for her to have "important information about a family member" she'd have to prove herself to me, first. I know all of Jean's past, except for two key factors: the identities of her birth mother and father. All we know is that they were from a small town, that her mother was younger, and that her father sounded like a typical small-town athlete. That's about all that she was ever able to find out. Is there the slightest possibility this "family member" might be one of them?

Nichole and I start out with the normal pleasantries when you exchange when you first speak with a stranger on the phone. I inform

Nichole that the letter struck us as a bit of a surprise—and suspicious. Guarded, I proceed to ask her, "What is this letter all about?" And I explain, "If you want to contact Jean, you will have to go through me first."

I start to grill Nichole about the letter and the family member that needs to get in touch with Jean. I ask, "Is this person alive? What state are they from? Is this person in jail? What is the urgency? Is someone dying—why is this person contacting her now?"

I stop at this point, realizing there is no sense in saying something I might regret in the future. The hair on the back of my neck is up, kind of like the way the hair stands up on a dog's shoulder when it gets really defensive. I still have no idea who Nichole is working for—or is representing.

At the end of our conversation, Nichole apologizes, saying, "I can't give you any information; however, there was another letter sent that might clear up some of your questions. I am sorry; I can't give you any more details."

Will this letter give me the answers to my questions, or will it create more questions? I don't know; we'll see.

Another letter arrives in the mail the day after I speak with Nichole. It has the same hand-written address on the envelope as before, so I open up the letter to see what was written. It contains the same text as before, but this time the letter is written on letterhead and there is a return address on the envelope. This gives me more to go on than the P.O. Box on the last letter. I know the street, Eustis Avenue, since Jean and I lived in a small apartment off that street when we were first married. I know Eustis Avenue pretty well between the streets of Larpenteur and Como Avenue, in St. Paul. A church, a parking lot, a bus stop, and Lutheran Social Services are pretty much all you'll find there. Could this be the place, and could someone actually be looking for Jean? I look the address up online and come up with Lutheran Social Services. I'm still not 100% convinced, so I call the Lutheran Social Services main number and ask for Nichole. The receptionist says she's not sure Nichole is in, but rings her extension: two rings and then the same familiar voice message. I'm almost certain that this might have something to do with a genetic relative—who, I don't know.

That evening, Jean and I discuss the matter at great lengths. I tell Jean of my investigation and tell her that I think the letter is legitimate. Even so, I've got a lot of questions for her. Why now—after all these years—might your parents or someone try to find you? If it was one of them, what do they look like? Might they live in Minnesota or nearby? Might you have siblings? I keep all of those to myself, though, and ask Jean, "Do you really want to find out?"

She says, "I'll think about it," but I can tell she is hesitant. "You know, Andrew, this could be a survey or something like that as well. I suppose I won't know unless I call."

I put the opened letter on the side table and tell her, "Okay, take some time and think about it."

The next morning, I get an email from Jean at 11:17 AM; the subject line simply reads, "*I called.*" I open up the email and read, "*I am shocked and so surprised!!!! I am in tears. How can I possibly work now?*"

Holy cow, she called Nichole! I can only imagine the conversation between the two. I sit nervously wondering what message I'll get next.

Half an hour later, at 11:43 AM, she emails me the shock of my life:

Hi – Nichole read me a letter that both my birth mother AND birth father wrote together. They got married last year.....it's sooooo sweet. I am incredibly teary now today because of this. It's so much more emotional for me than I ever anticipated it to be. She is sending me the letter with a picture of the two of them in the mail. I will let you read it. I never in my wildest imagination ever thought this would be the outcome of that letter that Nichole sent. Gosh.....

After I read her message and let it sink in for a minute, I respond with: "Holy Shit! "

"*I KNOW . . . I AM TOTALLY FREAKING OUT. This is so unexpected..... I can't stop crying,*" Jean replies.

The letter and photo from her birth parents is being sent to Jean this afternoon from Nichole. I'm a bit apprehensive, but I'm curious as to whom she might look like—and hoping for, perhaps, an explanation.

A few days pass before their letter and photo arrives.

I pick up the mail, but this is one letter that I wouldn't be opening. I know Jean never felt the need to find out who her birth parents were, but, for thirty-two years, I secretly did. Jean gets home from work and walks into the kitchen, where I left the unopened letter on the island for her to see. I am washing the deck with the hose, and I see her come to the deck door.

I tell her, "The letter has arrived." A look of nervous foreboding washes over her face. "You know I can open it for you if you want," I tell her.

"No, this is one letter I have to open myself," she says.

She shuts the door and sits down to open the envelope, and I let her digest all this information while I continue to wash the deck. She comes to the door and calls me to come into the house. I can tell she has been crying. We sit down in the kitchen club chairs, and she hands me the envelope. With trembling hands, Jean takes a deep breath and slowly opens the package to pull out the contents. I have a feeling in my stomach that this might not be good. You know how they say a picture is worth a thousand words? We were about to find out.

Jean pulls out the letter and the photo. She stares at the picture for a minute. A tear runs down her face, and she clutches the photo close to her chest and takes a huge gasp of air. "I finally look like someone!" she exclaims as she hands me the photo. The photo is of a well-dressed older couple holding each other in a heartfelt, loving manner. From the clothing they each are wearing, you can make some pretty good assumptions that they are educated and professionally employed. I study the picture to see if I can detect certain physical characteristics between mother and father and their daughter, my wife. I look at Jean and then the picture again. You can tell with absolute certainty that Jean is their daughter.

I get a chance to read the letter myself as Jean contemplates the picture of her birth parents. The letter is very well written, considering that it is also incredibly succinct. In a one-page letter, Jean's birth mother and father summed up fifty-four years of each of her parents' histories and their future plans, and expressed a willingness to meet, if we so chose. After reading that they wanted to move to a warmer state in the west, Jean questions what would be the point of meeting and then trying to work on some kind of long-distance relationship. To meet and then have them basically walk out like that might be more than Jean can handle.

I really think Jean has some reservations concerning that comment in the letter about moving west. I tell her that it doesn't appear to be set in stone, and that her parents did state in the letter that they would like to meet and "that there will be no negative feelings if you decide not to respond to this letter or contact us."

I re-read the letter again. There is a strong undertone that they really just want to know that Jean is alive and well. Three statements from the letter resonate the loudest for me. The first is: "We found each other again and now want to make our family complete." The other sentences that state "we think of you often" and "Know that you are loved," say a lot with few words. I can sense from the letter that there is a deep longing to bring some kind of closure to the questions they have asked each other for years—and to bring them some peace of mind.

I say to Jean, "We could meet once, and then take it day by day. We wouldn't make or set any expectations, just one day at a time. If we are to meet, that is a decision that you alone have to make.

A few days pass while we have some time to discuss the pros and cons, and I can tell Jean is waffling between calling Nichole back or not.

Last night I told Jean, "It'll be a big leap, but as long as we take it a day at a time on building whatever relationship you want out of this, then you owe it to yourself to call Nichole and see if they want to meet."

I am at work, and I just got an email from Jean. She writes, "*Well, Andrew, Nichole and I have just spoken on the phone. We chatted. My heart is pounding. The date has been set.*"

Chapter 24: 2016 – The Letter

Jean

I am deep in thought when I hear my husband, Andrew, say, "Jeanne, you got a letter in the mail today," and he hands it to me. I glance at it. It is a white envelope with a hand-written address and a return address of a P.O. Box. *Hmmmm.* My mind is on other things right now. I don't want to read it. So I set the envelope down on the lamp table between our chairs in the kitchen. He looks at me and asks, "Aren't you curious about what is in that letter?"

"No. Not really."

"Well you should read it. I already opened and read it, hope you don't mind," he says.

Soon after this exchange, Andrew gets up and leaves the room. I'm not necessarily thinking much about the letter, but I am curious enough to pick up the envelope and turn it over in my hands, looking for some kind of identification. There really isn't any. I take my finger and slide it under the unsealed flap and open it up. There is one single piece of paper in the envelope. I read the hand-written words, basically saying "I have some news about your family . . . ." Oh, for goodness' sake, I think to myself. Who has gotten into trouble now? It can't be my daughters because I would already know about it if it were them. What the heck is this? Looks like a scam.

Andrew walks into the room just as I put the letter back in the envelope and toss it on the side table.

"Well, Jean, what is it? What's this letter all about? Who do you think this is from?" he asks, looking at me and then down at the table.

"Ehh, seems like some kind of scam, Andrew. No big deal. You can deal with it, but I don't think it's much of anything."

He leans over and picks up the envelope, reading the contents of the letter for the second time. I look up from the iPad, where I have been looking something up on the Internet, and try to read his expression. I should have known it would be unreadable; that is just the way he is. I go back to searching.

"Are you going to call them?" he asks.

I don't even look up at him but sort of laugh and respond rather vehemently: "NO."

"Yeah, it does sound kind of fishy, doesn't it?" he asks. "Maybe you're right and it is some kind of scam." He pauses for a few moments and then turns to look at me and asks, "Do you mind if I call the number?"

"Why would you want to do that? Really? What's the point?"

"Just curiosity. Maybe you're right, and it is a scam, but what if it's not?"

"Andrew, you do what you want. I don't care. I don't have time for goofy stuff," I say. I really mean what I say. With work, being a mom, being a daughter, being a grandma and, of course, a wife, I don't feel like I have time to figure out whether something is a scam or not. I look up at him and smile. "You do such a good job of taking care of me that I will let you take care of this, too!"

That sentence gets him to smile, and he says, "I might call tomorrow. Now, what do you want for dinner? I got chicken or hamburger. You pick tonight."

"How about chicken stir fry?" I ask. "I will help cut up the vegetables."

The letter is not spoken of for the rest of the evening. I just let it go out of my mind. I have too many other things to worry about. We laugh about silly stuff while working together in the kitchen to make our chicken stir fry.

A couple of weeks later, I walk into the house after work, calling out, "Hi, Andrew, I am home." I stop and listen for a minute because I don't hear any response. I wonder where he is.

"Andrew, I'm home," I call out again.

"Up here. I'm in the TV room," I hear him call from upstairs.

I run upstairs and give him a quick peck on the cheek. "How was your day?" I ask.

He looks up from a piece of paper he has been reading and says, "My day was interesting. How was yours?"

I smile and say, "It was good. I had a lot of work to do today, but it was productive, and I got a lot done. My meetings went well, so I am happy about that. . . . Why was your day interesting?"

He peers at me over the top of his reading glasses and says, "I think you should sit down. I have something serious I want to talk to you about."

Seriously, in the last thirty-two years of marriage the man has never said those words to me. Ever! "Andrew, why do I need to sit down?"

"Remember that letter you got a couple of weeks ago? Well, you told me to take care of it, to deal with it. So I did. I think there is something you should know," he says quietly.

I slowly sink into the rocking chair that faces the couch. I sit on the edge and fold my hands in my lap. "Okay, I'm sitting. What is it that I couldn't stand for?" When I ask my question, my heart starts beating a little harder, and there is an inkling of something in the back of my mind—an inkling that I am not sure I can believe. My primary thoughts revolve around: My dad isn't sick, is he? There isn't something wrong with one of the girls, sons-in-law, or grandkids, is there? And then there is that tiny little inkling of a thought, but . . . no, it wouldn't be that.

"Jeanne, I think this letter is legit," he says, watching my face.

"What do you mean 'legit'?" I ask in a small, quiet voice, almost fearful.

"I called the number on the letter and, after doing some investigative work, I figured out the letter came from Children's Home Society/Lutheran Social Services."

"No. You're kidding, right? Andrew," I say in near-hysterics, "I am fifty-four years old. I am too old for someone to come looking for me. This is a joke."

"Sorry, I think it's the real deal. I think one of your parents has decided to find you. Maybe there is a reason for it."

"Like what, illness or hospitalization or something like that?"

"You never know—and you aren't going to know for sure unless you call this social worker, Nichole. I think you should call her and find out exactly what is going on. I tried to call for you and get some answers, but they are sworn by law to only speak with the adopted person. She will only speak with you," he says.

"Well, I am not calling her, Andrew. I can't open up this door if that is what it is. I have heard a lot of stories about adoption reunions gone badly. I don't want to hurt anyone, and I certainly do not want to be hurt. Don't you think we have enough drama with just normal life without inviting more drama into it?" I ask, practically panic-stricken.

"Calm down, Jean, you are just making a phone call to a counselor at the adoption agency. You aren't doing anything more. You are finding out what Lutheran Social Services wants. Maybe it isn't even a birth parent wanting to find you. Maybe it's some kind of survey they want to do with adopted children. You don't know unless you make the phone call," Andrew says calmly and logically. He looks at me then, and smiles. "You are just making a phone call. That's all."

I shake my head and walk into our bedroom to change out of my skirt into jeans and a t-shirt for the evening. I had been kind of hungry, and now my stomach is rolling with a light nausea. Thoughts are whirling through my head. I am conflicted because I want to know exactly why they are seeking me out right now—so I don't have to think about it anymore—but then I also don't want to call and find out what the agency really wants.

The evening goes by rather slowly. Andrew and I make supper; we chat and wash the dishes. I throw in a load of laundry, and by the time the dryer is done it is about 9:00. I go downstairs to get the load of towels, and, as I am folding them, Andrew comes into the kitchen and starts to fold them with me.

"I think you should call, Jean. You have been preoccupied tonight," he says.

"Okay, Andrew," I say hesitantly, not really wanting to commit, but knowing inside myself that I will probably call. Then I announce, "I am going to call my Dad just to see how he is doing."

I pick my cell phone up off the counter and dial my dad. I hear him pick up and say hello, "Hey, Dad," I exclaim in a chipper tone.

"Oh, hey, Jeanne girl, how are ya?"

"Pretty good, Dad. I was just checking in with you to make sure you were feeling okay."

He laughs and replies, "Just swell. Sharon and I are just sitting here watching basketball. I got done doing my exercises a few minutes ago, and now I am relaxing in my chair," he says. "How was work?" My dad remarried a few years back, and it is comforting to know he is just hanging out with Sharon during the evening hours.

"Work was good, Dad, but for some reason I felt like I should just call you. I had some kind of goofy premonition." I hesitate.

"Well, be reassured we are both fine here!"

We chat a bit more and then hang up. As I click the call off, I feel better. I had been uneasy at the beginning of the night, and just hearing Dad's voice made me feel calmer.

The next morning I sit and stare at the phone on my desk. I am exhausted since I didn't sleep—how could I, with all kinds of thoughts rolling around in my head? It's 7:30 AM, and I know the agency offices are not open, yet. *Do I want to call or not?* I know I do not want to call on my cell phone. *It would be better if the call came from a business,* I think. The time clicks slowly by, and I can't seem to concentrate on my work. The thought crosses my mind that if this is just a survey, I have wasted a lot of time worrying or dreading or being excited for absolutely nothing.

I call the number at 9:30 and the ring is answered by a friendly female voice.

"Hi, my name is Jean, and I received a letter from you a month ago or so," I slowly say.

"Well, Jean, thank you so much for calling me back. I did hear from your husband, but the nature of this call is such that I could only speak with you," the voice on the other end of the line says, then pauses. When I don't say anything, she continues, "We have received word from your birth parents, Jean. They are looking for you," she says, and then she waits.

This news leaves me confused. "My parents?"

"Yes, they are together and have decided to contact you. They had been apart and are now together." The counselor, Nichole, pauses again before she goes on. "They have written you a letter, Jean. Would you like me to read it to you?"

I sit for a moment, trying to digest the information. "You mean it's not just one parent looking for me; it's both?" I ask incredulously.

"Let me read you the letter; it will explain more for you," she clarifies.

"Yes, okay. . . . I think I'm ready. . . . Okay, read me the letter," I say rather breathlessly.

Nichole goes on to read the letter, and my eyes fill with tears as she reads. This certainly cannot be happening, can it? I am unsure of my emotions and how I feel. There is an excitement within me, but there is also an underlying thin thread of . . . fear. Nichole comes to a part of the letter that says my parents just got married in 2015, and I am stunned. My birth parents just got married. This is crazy, I think to myself. That doesn't happen every day. Then, at the end of the letter, there is another line that says that meeting me would make their family complete. Well that does it—the stupid dam of tears that had been a trickle suddenly becomes full-fledged crying. I have to get out of my cubicle and into the bathroom. For goodness' sake, I am at work!

Nichole is very kind, patient, and supportive and even expresses some empathy, "Take it easy, take a few breaths, and take your time." After a few breaths and a bit of silence, as she waits for me to compose myself, she inquires, "They have requested contact with you, Jean. Would you like to write them a letter? I can put this letter and the photos they have given me for you in an envelope and send it to you. The next step is up to you. You can think about it, take some time."

I'm not sure what to say, but I do want to see the pictures. I am curious and want to see if, after fifty-four years, I look like someone. I cautiously reply, "Yes, I would like to reread the letter and see their pictures. I am certainly interested and eager to see if I look like someone, finally." Then I give a nervous little laugh. I shake my head and wonder, Did that sound stupid? It may have.

"Great. I will put the package in the mail today, and, when you are ready, call me back and we can talk more about the next steps."

We end our conversation after a bit more small talk, and upon hanging up the phone I run to the bathroom, lock myself in a stall, and silently cry. I need to just let out all of my emotions—happiness, excitement, nervousness, and panic. Fifty-four years of the unknown, and now there are answers. Is this Pandora's box?

It takes a full week for the package with the letter and the pictures to get to me. *Seriously, why is it when you really want the mail to come—it doesn't? Please explain this to me.* This particular day, I have a premonition that the package is going to be on the kitchen island when I get home. I walk into the house and call Andrew's name, but he is outside power-washing the deck. Glancing at the island in the kitchen, half afraid to look—thinking I will be disappointed if it isn't there—I see a large white envelope with my name on it. My heart is racing. There is the envelope I have been waiting for all week.

I open up the deck door to say hello to Andrew. He looks at me, slows down the water and says with a smile, "Your letter arrived."

"Do you want to come into the house, take a break and open it with me?" I ask.

"No," he replies, "I want you to do this on your own. You open the letter, read it, and then—when you're ready—I will come in and we can chat. Sound okay?"

"Yes, okay, that's a good idea," I weakly acknowledge. Already I can feel my eyes start to sting, and I haven't even done anything, yet. Good grief!

Andrew goes back to his task while I shut the door and walk over to the envelope. I stare at it for a little bit. I am excited, nervous, uneasy, happy, and eager. It is crazy to have all of those emotions swirling around in the pit of my stomach. I think of my dad, wondering what he would say if he were standing here with me. I am seeing him in three days to tell him the story. I called him earlier this week and told him I was coming to visit him, thinking that I was going to talk to him about this letter.

As I sit down in my leather chair, my hands are kind of shaking and my insides feel hot and cold all at the same time. I pick up the envelope, open it, and pull out the contents. There is some paperwork from Children's Home Society, an envelope labeled "photos," and then the letter. Even though I want to see the photos, I wait. I very slowly and purposefully read the letter twice and take in all the words that had been read to me a week earlier. I smile to myself and feel a weird . . . connection. It is very hard to describe, but there is something in me that just feels warmth.

I open the envelope of photos, and the first one is a picture of two people smiling into the camera. My eyes fill with tears. Of course they would. The first thought I have as I look at this picture is: I look like someone—I look like my father. I pull out the other two photos, one photo each of my birth parents separately, and I notice my mother's smile—it's my smile. All of a sudden I am overwhelmed. I just start to sob. My shoulders shake, and my chest feels like an elephant is sitting on it.

I take a few minutes to let everything kind of soak in. I read the letter again, look at the pictures, and walk over to the deck door.

"I read it," I announce to my husband.

"I can see," his eyes widen with his smile.

"Do you want to read it?" I ask in a small, tight voice.

He looks at me and comes back with, "Of course. Let me turn the water off, and I will be right in."

After he comes into the house, he sits down in his chair and takes the envelope and its contents from me. He reads everything and then looks at the pictures. "You look like your mother; you have her smile," he expresses with a grin.

"Do you really think so?" I ask. "I kind of think I am a perfect mix of the two of them." I can tell that I'm beaming. "The social worker said on the phone that they want to meet me. What is your opinion of that? Would you meet them if you were in my shoes?"

"Jeanne, it's your decision, but if you really want my opinion, I think you should meet them. Write them a letter and give them some dates that you and I are free and we can go meet them," his voice is calm and reassuring.

I don't respond right away because I am processing everything, but a few minutes later I speak up and say, "I know I will want to meet them, but let me think about this for a little bit." And I turn around and walk upstairs to my office. As I sit down at my desk, my thoughts are tumbling around in my mind. One thought keeps surfacing: My life could really change.

Dinner conversation that night mostly focuses around feelings and a reiteration of many conversations we have already had over the last week. I am exhausted and can hardly keep my eyes open any more. *Maybe I will finally sleep.*

I had started a letter to my birth parents early the previous Friday morning after the Thursday phone call with the social worker. Now, a week later, as I sit in my home office with a cup of coffee two hours before I actually start work (I usually work from home on Fridays), I think I am ready to finish the letter, now that I have seen their pictures and read their letter again.

Sitting down to write, I feel excitement and am overwhelmed with emotion. I feel that by responding to their letter, my life may change—that my life *will* change. I think this might be the longest hand-written correspondence I have ever written, and I smile to myself as I start to write my thoughts.

A couple of days later, we are celebrating my daughter's birthday. I want her day to be special, and I am focusing all of my efforts and attention on her—or at least I think I am. My four grandchildren are running around, so I keep getting sidetracked with what they are doing, and my mind is simply not allowing me to relax. Andrew and I had decided earlier that, after the birthday celebration, we are going to tell the family about the letter from my birth parents.

The day has been a lovely day of celebration, and I can see my family starting to get tired—especially my daughter, who is eight months pregnant and eager to go home to get some rest before work the next morning.

Looking at her, I implore, "Can you hold off for ten minutes? I want to have a little family gathering in the living room."

She gives me a weak smile and says, "Really, Mom, are you sure we have to do this tonight?"

I quickly respond, "Yeah, I know you are tired, and I promise to try and keep it brief. You know I want you to get your rest. Let's gather the family and go into the living room,"

I take a few minutes and gather the family. Since we are celebrating my daughter Laura's birthday, a lot of family has gathered to celebrate her day. I look around and take a quick mental roll call. My dad and Sharon couldn't make it today. My brother, William, lives in Dallas, so he doesn't get to come to family birthday parties very often. Andrew's dad has just gotten into his pickup and is driving down the driveway. It is my immediate family that is left.

My oldest daughter, Terra, her husband, Aaron, and their children are there. Birthday girl Laura and her husband, Joe, and my youngest daughter, Hanna, are gathered in the living room. There are some questioning looks on their faces, and I can tell they are wondering why I have called them all together. My stomach is uneasy, and I am feeling jittery. The hand in which I'm holding the letter is trembling.

"I know you are all anxious to get home, but before you leave I want to read you a letter I received in the mail this week." I pause and then begin reading, "Dear Daughter, . . ." I continue to read the letter, and when I start to tear up, I look at Andrew and say, "I don't think I can read anymore."

He responds quickly, "Yes, you can. It's your story; now finish the letter."

I continue to read through tears that are glistening on my lashes. When I reach the part in the letter where Karen and Dennis have written ". . . we'd like to make our family complete . . ." I break down with small hiccupping sobs and finish reading. When I reach the end, I look at my three daughters, and they all have tears in their eyes and on their cheeks. "They are your grandparents, girls. What do think? How do you feel? Should I meet them?"

All three of them get up and surround me in a group hug. Then the rest of the family joins them. There are questions and answers, but they all encourage me to meet my birth parents, and they, too, want to meet their grandparents. After a bit more conversation, the family leaves Andrew and me for their homes. I am weary. It has certainly been one emotional day, and, as I lay my head on the pillow, I am exhausted and drift off to sleep.

The following Saturday morning I decide to tell my dad and his wife, Sharon, that I have been contacted by my birth parents. I drive to Hayfield to see them and am actually nervous when I pull into the driveway and face the house. My thoughts are jumbled because I am trying to formulate how I want to tell my dad this news. I am unsure of how he is going to respond. Opening the front door, I walk into the foyer and call out, "Hi, it's just me."

"Well, hello there," my dad responds.

I can hear Sharon in the kitchen calling out her own "Hello, Jean." I give both of them a hug in greeting, and we settle into the kitchen around the little island. We make some general small talk at the beginning of the conversation, and then I feel like I just need to get the conversation over. My stomach is in knots, I am nervous, and my hands start shaking. I've brought the letter from Dennis and Karen along with me, and I decide that maybe it's best to just read it to them.

"So," I say, and then I pause to take a deep breath, "I received a letter in the mail a couple of weeks ago from Lutheran Social Services." I pause again because I want to watch my dad's face. His eyebrows go up, but he doesn't say anything, so I continue. "The letter was sent by a social worker, and we ended up having a conversation by phone. She explained that my birth parents have decided to look for me, mainly to know if I am alive and well. They have sent a letter and are requesting a chance to meet me. I'd like to read the letter to you, Dad, if you are okay with that."

"Sure, sure go ahead," he replies.

I look at him to see his eyes. They are masked, and he is quiet. I can't read them, or what he is thinking, but I don't want to ask either. I am afraid of hurting him and am hoping I have not opened up a wound of the past. I look at Sharon, and she nods her head. So I decide to read the letter. I read the words and get a little teary in parts as I read it aloud. When I end, I stop and wait—waiting to see what they have to say.

Dad nods his head and suggests, "Well, I guess you have a decision to make. You don't have to see them. Don't feel like you have to meet them."

"What if I tell you that I want to meet them?" I reply.

"Do you really want to meet them? Are you just curious?" he asks.

"Yes, actually I do. I have talked about it a lot with Andrew and have given it much thought. I wrote them a letter and told them in the letter that I would meet them."

"You have no obligation to them, Jean," he says with a smile. "You will always be my daughter—and don't you ever forget that."

"Oh, Dad, of course I would never forget that. I don't even know if they want more than just to meet me," I say reassuringly. "You will always be my dad." I smile at him and get up to wrap my arms around his neck from behind and give him a quick kiss on the cheek.

Dad looks at me and smiles and gives his approval, but it is given with a hint of reservation.

"You won't call him 'Dad' will you?"

"No, for goodness' sake, Dad. . . . That is a name of familiarity, and that is what I call you. I may use another respectful name though. I haven't actually thought about it, so I guess we have to see what happens." As I say this out loud the thought I have is, I could call Dennis "Father" and Karen "Mother" and that way I can keep Dad, Mom, Father and Mother all separate.

Sharon voices her support, and we continue to talk a little bit more about the letter. I then ask, "Would you ever want to meet them, Sharon?"

"Yes, I would meet them," she says, but she doesn't say more.

I turn and look at my dad and ask, "How about you, Dad? Would you be willing to meet them?"

He thinks about his answer before speaking and then says, "No, I don't think so. Not right now. Now is not the time. Maybe someday I will, but not right now."

Sharon asks me, "How are you handling all of this? Are you dealing with new emotions?"

I look at both of them and respond thoughtfully, "There aren't any real negative emotions—except for maybe some fear."

"Fear of what?" Sharon asks.

"Maybe fear of rejection, or fear that I am not good enough," I say.

"We know you are sensitive, Jean, but you gotta get over that," my dad says with a slightly irritated tone of voice. "You don't have anything to fear from getting to know people. Just be yourself."

"Your dad is right, Jean. They will accept you for who you are. If they don't, you still have a lot of people in your life that love you," Sharon says with emotion. "You are a wonderful daughter."

"I wanted to talk to both of you because I feel kind of guilty wanting to meet them," I say in a tremulous voice, looking down at my trembling hands. "I have to admit there are emotions. There are many thoughts surfacing about who I am. I think a lot about stories of other people who have met their birth parents. Some stories don't always have a happy ending.

Sharon looks at me and says, "You have a strong family bond. You will be fine. You might be a little overwhelmed, but I think that is normal."

"Jean, just take it one day at a time. That is all we can do," my dad says in a matter-of-fact tone of voice, and then he smiles at me. "Just don't forget about me, okay?"

We continue our conversation, but we switch to other subjects. The nerves in my belly disappear, and my hands stop shaking. I am feeling at peace. I am glad I told them and was upfront about it. I had actually entertained the idea of not telling my dad, but I am really glad I did—better to be up front and honest.

Honesty, I learned at a very early age in life, is the key to the harmonization of human beings in general. I laugh out loud when I think of this last statement. It just reminds me of when I was ten years old and telling the biggest whopper of my life.

Chapter 25: 2016 – May 31, 2016

Jean

Staring into my closet, I can't find anything I want to wear. Everything is too . . . *something*. It's either too bright, too dull, too small, too big . . . . "Good grief!" I say out loud to no one. I really need to calm down and find some clothes. I flip through everything again, for the fourth time. Today is a special day. It will be a day that will go down in my own little history. This day may change my life, and I am well aware of that fact. It makes me very apprehensive. Today, I am supposed to meet the mother and father who gave me life. This is almost too much for my mind to really grasp.

"Andrew!" I scream almost hysterically, "I don't have anything to wear!"

He looks at me with a big grin and says, "You have plenty of clothes. Wear something conservative. Wear something I like."

Typical of him to say that, I stare at him with a tiny bit of exasperation, "Then tell me what to wear."

All Andrew does is turn his attention to his own wardrobe and ignore my request with a little grin on his face. I pull out of the closet a salmon-colored, soft, silky blouse and appreciate the fit and the way it feels. I had passed by it before because I thought the color was too bright, but maybe it will be okay for today. Maybe it will give a bit of blush to my face since I look so pasty white after the long Minnesota winter. When I put it up to my face, so I can see it in the mirror, I see Andrew's reflection and notice his nod of approval. Good. We got a shirt nailed down. Next item?

I'm nervous and feel nauseated. I can't eat anything, I didn't sleep last night, I can't find the right clothes, shoes are always an issue with me (Do you think they would mind if I was barefoot?) and I feel like my husband is laughing at me with the silly grin he is wearing. I pace the floor and get really mad when my hair won't curl the way I want. Whenever I am worked up about anything, my hair never turns out the way I think it should. Why is that? Why in the world does the crazy hair thing always happen to me? Do other people have these kinds of issues, or is it only me? My assumption is that today, of all the people in the world, it is only me who is having these issues. It is probably normal. I give a huge audible sigh.

Seriously—this is probably the most emotional thing I have gone through in my adult life. But . . . well . . . maybe not the most. My parents' divorce might have been the worst. Then my logical brain remembers when my mother passed away. Of course that was emotional. However, this situation is aggravatingly complicated, moving, and poignant. Yes, this is emotional and ranks right up there. What if they don't like me? How does a person deal with two families? What if they just want to have a conversation and not a relationship? What if they want a relationship?

The last two weeks have brought about feelings I have suppressed all these years. As I look at my reflection in the mirror, I smile. I may be nervous, but I am happy, too. "Excited" seems too calm of an adjective for my mental state. I desire to meet the people who brought me into existence and to hear the story of their lives. I want to know all about them. I want to know what makes them delighted or sad. I want to know what kind of music they enjoy. I want to know what kind of food they like to eat. Are they social people? Do they like nature? I want to know what they like to do for fun . . . both now and what they did together in the past. But I do not know where I want this "meeting" to go. I do not know what I want at the end of the day. I do not know if I want a relationship. What if I feel no connection to these people? There are so many complicated emotions racing at breakneck speed around my brain, that I am having a hard time even putting them into words.

Chapter 26: 2016 – Our First Meeting, May 31, 2016

Dennis

We wrote a letter to the daughter we have yet to meet, that started with "Dear Daughter" explaining the situation and how we chose adoption. We received a five-page follow-up letter to us where we found out her name is now "Jean," and she thanked us for choosing adoption over abortion. She also gave us four dates that were available for her and her husband to meet us at Lutheran Social Services with our case worker as a mediator.

May 31, 2016, at 10:00 AM, was the first date listed, so we chose to meet at that time. We found out, later, she was reluctant to meet, and so were we. Halfway up the stairs to the office, we almost turned around. However, we decided to go through with it, and we are glad we did.

When we walk into the room, it is a very emotional reception: a daughter seeing her biological mother and father for the first time, and the parents seeing their daughter after fifty-four years. After an hour or so of sharing photos and family information, her husband, Andrew—still concerned for his wife's emotional state—makes the comment to us, "If you just meet Jean and then disappear again, it would devastate her."

We have the room for an hour and a half, from 10:00 to 11:30, and from there we go to a restaurant called the Monte Carlo in Minneapolis for a three-hour lunch. During lunch, I have a hard time remembering her name is Jean and call her "Denise" a few times because I am so accustomed to thinking about her with that name.

We do not want the day to end. After we establish that we are going to keep a relationship with our daughter, within one day's time,

Karen and I go from four kids between the two of us to five. We also go from six grandkids to nine grandkids—and from no great-grand-kids to five.

We have no regrets. Now we all live our separate lives—but together as family.

I realize that my communication with Karen has become strength-ened through our electronic courtship and the experience of finding Jean. We have made a commitment to each other to be honest and truthful in our relationship and to enjoy the love we have for each other in the remaining years we have together.

Chapter 27: 2016 – Our Family Completed, May 31, 2016

Karen

E ven though our meeting date, May 31, 2016, was only a few days away, our excitement was overwhelming. Occasionally, however, the question arose, "Are we really doing the right thing in meeting Jean? After all, she has her own family. Why would she want to meet us after all these years?"

We nearly turn around while driving to Lutheran Social Services but feel that since we have come so far, we might as well continue with the meeting—regardless of the outcome.

We are greeted at the reception desk of Lutheran Social Services and ushered up the stairs. My heart is pounding as I nervously grasp Dennis's hand. The door opens and there is Jean with a radiant smile just like Dennis's smile. We hug and cry. The rest of the meeting—and beyond—is spent sharing old photos and stories about our families and our past. It is great, and we don't want it to end.

Jean and her husband, Andrew, extend an invitation for us to join their family for a celebration in four days—an invitation that we cannot turn down. We now have an additional three granddaughters, and five great-grandchildren.

The succeeding months are filled with joy, getting to know our extended family. Thanksgiving 2016 is extra special as several of our out-of-town children and grandchildren come to visit and are able to meet their "new" sister and brother-in-law—and aunt, uncle, and new cousins.

The year 2016, in our memories, will always be a year filled with anticipation and excitement. Not only did we find our daughter and increase our family size, we decided to move to Northfield, Minnesota, from Eden Prairie—an idea suggested by our "new" daughter, who lives about twenty miles from Northfield. My original thought had been that, once we sold the house and property in Washington—where I had lived for eighteen years—we would finally live in a warmer climate. (Dennis once owned a home in Palm Desert, California, which he liked, but in my research, I preferred northern Arizona.) However, in a conversation with Jean one day, she asked, "Have you considered moving to Northfield?"

"No," we replied. "What does Northfield have to offer?"

"Well, it's close to Andrew and me, but aside from that, it has two colleges, it's only forty-nine minutes from Orchestra Hall in Minneapolis (something Dennis likes especially well), and it has small-town charm with not a lot of traffic."

We visit Northfield in July to find it is everything she said it was—plus more. So we start looking for townhomes. We discover that Northfield was rated the "most popular retirement community in Minnesota" by Money Magazine in 2014. So the movers are called and our belongings are transported from Monroe, Washington, and Eden Prairie, Minnesota, to Northfield. Combining two households in the new townhome we selected is no small feat.

"If I would have known you were such high maintenance, Karen, I would not have asked you to marry me," Dennis teases me to this day.

One negative thing of living in Northfield is that we have moved farther away from Dennis's youngest son, daughter-in-law, and three grandchildren, who also live in Minnesota. With the rest of Dennis's children living on the west coast, we enjoy spending time with the closer children, watching sporting events, musicals, and theatrical productions—as well as celebrating holidays and birthdays. The increased driving distance limits our visits now, more than we'd like. My son also lives in Washington state, so we don't see each other often.

Our daughter said that, throughout her life, she often wondered if she looked like anyone. It is uncanny what hereditary traits transfer from one generation to another. Examples in our circumstance not only reflect facial features—like Jean's eyes and nose that look like her father's, and her mouth, which is like mine. We have also discovered that some interests are inherited. As a child, Jean liked to design costumes for her paper dolls and draw floor plans—she even considered going to New York to be a fashion designer—and always wondered why she had an artistic talent for costume design.

Her tastes in clothes are also similar to ours, but one outstanding incident occurred when Dennis and I were going through several fabric books from an upholstery shop to select fabric for two chairs and a sofa for our living room in our new Northfield home. Out of several hundred swatches in the books, Dennis and I selected a solid color for the sofa and a subtle geometric pattern for the two chairs. Without telling her our choices, we handed all of the fabric books to Jean and asked her to select fabric for our furniture. To our surprise, she selected the exact same fabric as we had chosen. We all looked in amazement at each other. Andrew was in disbelief and thought it was rigged.

Another trait she inherited from her father was her ability to relate to people. And did I mention that she also has inherited her father's restless leg condition?

My experience in reconnecting with and marrying my junior high and high school sweetheart, plus finding Jean after all these years, has deepened my spiritual faith that God cares for me and loves me.

Epilogue: Happily Ever After
Jean

Thanksgiving 2016

This Thanksgiving is definitely a holiday to celebrate. I look back on 2016 and realize I have many things for which to be thankful. Of course there are the obvious things: Andrew, my daughters, my sons-in-law, and my grandchildren. But then there are other people, things, and events to be thankful for this year: my parents, new aunts and uncles, and new siblings—whom I have met during this glorious Thanksgiving holiday week.

A year ago I never dreamed I would have new parents and siblings with whom to celebrate a holiday. This has been such a delightful week. It's been wonderful because of the new relationships that are now a part of my life: new siblings, sisters-in-law, nieces, and nephews. Andrew, our daughters, and their families were all welcomed into a new chapter of life. It's been so fantastic to have conversations on Thanksgiving Day with my new siblings. I have watched my daughters laugh at something that an aunt, uncle, or cousin said. Somehow I have managed to keep it together and enjoy this amazing Thanksgiving week, which has been filled with celebratory activities and getting to know my new family.

My brother, William, came home to Minnesota for a visit in October. We had made plans by phone to spend some time together, and he was going to stay at our house for the duration of his stay.

Andrew and I were meeting my birth parents at a restaurant called The Depot in Faribault, Minnesota, which is about fifteen miles from our home in Kenyon. Andrew and I were sitting at the bar, having a soda water and cranberry juice, waiting for my parents to arrive. When I saw them walk through the door, I got excited and met both of them with a hug. The hostess came to take my parents to a table to be seated while I walked back to the bar to grab my drink.

I grabbed the glass off the bar and glanced towards the door. I had to blink twice. It was my brother! What in the world is he doing here? I thought incredulously. I wasn't expecting to see him until Andrew and I got home that night.

I get up from the bar stool and run over to him to give him a big "hello" hug. I look at him and exclaim, "It is so good to see you, William, but what are you doing here?"

"I arrived in town and was hungry. I have always liked The Depot, so I came over here before I drove over to your house." He smiles back at me. "What are you doing here? I thought you were going to go to a concert in town tonight?"

"Andrew and I decided to grab some food with my parents before the concert."

"Your parents?" he asks with a questioning look.

"Yes, my birth parents. I want you to meet them. Please?"

"Oh, I don't want to bother you. I will talk to you more when you get home."

"Oh, you should have dinner with us," I say to him.

"No, I don't want to intrude. You and I can talk later."

"William, come on. Let me introduce you."

We walk over to the table, and I say with a wide smile on my face, "Parents, I want to introduce you to my brother, William." I make the introductions and then ask them if they care if he joins us. Happily, they say they don't mind, and the five of us have a lovely dinner together. I explain to my parents that in order to communicate with William the best, they have to look him in the eye and speak slowly so he can lip read. After the initial awkwardness of introducing my brother to my birth parents, the conversation goes smoothly.

We talk about the Twins and the Vikings. William asks about the girls and conversation seems to flow rather well. I think they all are enjoying meeting one another. After dinner, William goes back to my house, and my parents, Andrew, and I go to the concert.

184

The next day, William and I are chatting about the evening, and he says to me, "You are lucky, Jean. You have found your birth parents, and they are kind people. Not every adopted person gets a chance to have this kind of meeting and then a relationship with their biological family. I am kind of envious. I would like to meet my own birth parents. I would like to meet them and ask them my own questions."

I agree with William that I am one of the fortunate ones, and I do feel blessed. My dad and Sharon have also been supportive. He has listened and offered advice when I have discussed the new people and relationships I have in my life. I think of this now, as I contemplate all the relationships in my life. There are new and existing connections with people that make me realize how delightful life can be.

This week, I am not in a place of sadness, grief, and gloom—a place I have been often within the past three years. During that time, there have been days when I have not been able to pull myself out of it, but this week my spirits are lifted. Sadness and grief have taken a back seat. They are around, but definitely not sitting in the front seat with me. I miss my mom, but I have to admit that the grief has been more manageable this year. I know it gets easier to deal with grief in time (I read that in my grief book), but I also feel that after meeting my parents and siblings this week, maybe that has something to do with it, as well.

Have you ever asked yourself, "Is your life what you imagined?" It's an interesting question. I have pondered this during my drive time to the Twin Cities. It's an easy thing to think about when you are alone with your thoughts on the road in front of you. No, my life is not what I had imagined it would be, or what I thought it would be, but life has a way of making itself evolve with every decision that you make. There are forks in the road where you can make a choice. Both options might be good . . . but they may have different results. When I got pregnant in college, I did have an important choice to make. My birth mother also had her own life-impacting choice to make. I chose to move forward and have my child—and what a blessing she has been. What a blessing *all three* of my children have been to Andrew and me. They are the greatest decisions a mother could ever make.

Thinking about my mom and dad, and what it must have been like to be twenty-two years old and told they would never have children, I think it must have been hard on my mom—and my dad. Mom might have been devastated. We didn't talk much about it, but she did say it was hard to hear that she would never bear a child. I was a gift: Karen gave my mom the gift of a life. It comes back around. I may still grieve my sweet mom, but I also have a chance to be a daughter to the mother who gave me life.

When I think of a fifteen-year-old girl having to make the decision to either have or give up a child, it gives me chills up and down my arms—because I was that baby. My birth mother blocked out some of the pain from her memory, which is only natural. But then, years later, Mother and Father made the decision to find their child. That is a miracle, isn't it?

Life is going to play out the way it should. There is a bigger picture. I truly believe that there are reasons why we make the decisions that we do, and that no matter which road we take God can work with us and help us along the way. My birth parents searching and finding their daughter only goes to show me that we were meant to have some time together—maybe not a lifetime, but enough time to be blessings to one another.

May 31, 2017 – Our First Anniversary

Tonight, we celebrated our first anniversary together. Tonight we celebrated love that was once lost but now again is found. Fifty years of love lost, then found, in a couple of different ways: my birth parents' own love story, and then "our" love story, where I am included.

Isn't that brilliant? Isn't it wonderful to have an incredible experience where you can live your life, enjoy your life, and also have the ability to obtain the most valuable thing we can have in this life: love? And imagine that it is love that you had, then lost, due to life's circumstances—but then it came back around full circle, fifty years later. Now that is something to celebrate—and I am ecstatic that I can bear witness to that kind of love and then be a part of it.

That is "happily ever after." That is the most perfect present, a unique kind of gift that only God can give.

Epilogue: Expect a Miracle
Dennis

The book you have just read has been a labor of love for all of us.

As we walk out the service door into the garage in our Northfield home, above the door is a plaque that reads "Expect a Miracle." The miracle started in 2014 when I found Karen, my first love, and we decided to find our daughter, Jean, on May 31, 2016. This miracle can only be a gift from God.

My life has encountered many twists and turns along the way as I have chosen one path over another. However, there have been many lessons learned over my lifetime. One affirmation that I believe can be credited to Ernie Larson, a motivational speaker whom I admire, is: "What you live with, you learn; what you learn, you practice; what you practice, you become." As I look back to my younger years, this holds true when I was learning and developing my work ethics and emotions from my mother.

My strong loving and caring personality has not always been a blessing. I hurt and am saddened easily, as can be seen in my reactions to losing Karen and giving up my first-born daughter. I can also associate part of my drinking alcohol on my inability to say "No," which in turn affected my relationship in my first marriage and succeeding relationships with several other women. After going to therapy for seven years to learn how to say "No" to people, I was finally able to comfortably share my feelings and experiences with people. It was through therapy that I made many close friends from all walks of life.

For twenty-five years, I volunteered at Hennepin County Workhouse in Minneapolis holding talks specifically focusing on Alcoholics Anonymous and drug abuse.

After thirty-three years of sobriety, you learn to forgive, but not necessarily forget. One piece of advice on which I still rely today came from my psychologist: "Don't explain; don't defend; don't attack."

I am very favored to have four wonderful children of my own, as well as Karen's son, as family. Karen and I are blessed with a very large family now. I feel very fortunate.

Acknowledgments

This book is a special, intimate journey of the heart by the four of us. Our hearts are full of love and gratitude for the people who have helped us in the creation of this memoir. Many people have supported us in the several months and multiple drafts it took to complete this manuscript.

A special thank you goes to Julie and Jim Vinar for your generosity and patience, for taking the time to read through the story several times, and for giving us such valuable feedback. Our gratitude goes out to Barb Vinar and Amy Vinar for your analysis of the way the story flows and for giving us some wonderful direction and support. We express our thanks to Laura Walter, Karen Jurgenson, and other family members for offering their insight, evaluating the story, and making suggestions. We give thanks for the support of Terra Haugen, Hanna Voxland, and several women of Lambda Delta Phi, who listened to our story and offered their ideas.

CPSIA information can be obtained
at www.ICGtesting.com
Printed in the USA
LVOW13s0858020118
561499LV00019B/330/P

9 781545 617106